MEMOIRS OF AN AVERAGE ANGLER

JUST ME
AND
THE FISH

"IT'S NOT THE FISH YOU CAUGHT THAT
MAKES YOU RETURN,
BUT THE FISH YOU DIDN'T CATCH"

Mereo Books

1A The Wool Market Dyer Street Cirencester Gloucestershire GL7 2PR
An imprint of Memoirs Publishing www.mereobooks.com

Just Me and the Fish

978-1-86151-919-1

First published in Great Britain in 2019
by Mereo Books, an imprint of Memoirs Publishing

Copyright ©2019

Mike Fox has asserted his right under the Copyright Designs and Patents Act 1988 to be identified as the author of this work.

Every effort has been made to obtain copyright permissions for the use of the illustrations in this book, however it has not always been possible to trace copyright holders. Any concerns with regard to copyright should be address to the publishers, who will be pleased to respond appropriately

The address for Memoirs Publishing Group Limited can be found at www.memoirspublishing.com

The Memoirs Publishing Group Ltd Reg. No. 7834348

Typeset in 9/12pt Bembo

by Wiltshire Associates Publisher Services Ltd.
Printed and bound in Great Britain by Biddles Books

CONTENTS

FOREWORD

Fishing or angling: whatever you call it it's all the same to me, but it's not to everyone's liking. Many people will have their own perception of what I and millions of others see as a wonderful pastime, or sport as it's now officially categorised with Sport England. Statistics suggest that angling boasts the highest number of individual sporting participants in the UK, while others will suggest that numbers are in a slow decline. Whatever the numbers, the consensus is that the sport is an intriguing activity that can at times be surprisingly physically and mentally demanding.

But do non-anglers really understand what fishing/angling is truly all about? When I ask non-anglers about their perception of our sport, they more often than not reply "well, it's very boring" and say they can't think of anything less exciting than watching a piece of plastic bobbing about on the water for hours on end just waiting for a fish to take the bait. Others feel they don't have the inclination to pursue such a sedentary, time-consuming activity. Some will say they have never taken the opportunity and have only ever watched it on TV. Many people say they do not have the patience and it would be a total waste of their valuable time. Maybe so, but it requires more concentration than patience.

These misconceptions are, in my mind, no reason for anyone not to try out the sport. There is that element of inactivity at times when the fish just will not bite, that's inevitable, but there are many other aspects of angling worth exploring. Any angler will agree that most of the time spent fishing doesn't actually involve contact with fish. It's a time when you can experience nature in a way that is impossible any other way. You will see things that most people never will and hear things that many people will ignore. You will feel things that many people will never touch, and smell things that other people can't. It is those moments within an aquatic world you can bond with that make you realise that it's not the fish you caught which makes you return, but the fish you didn't catch.

This book is a journey through my experiences, incorporating an anthology of coarse and game angling adventures through the years, and telling from how I first developed an interest in coarse angling at the age of seven to the present-day joys of fly-fishing. It is not another instruction manual, I'll leave that to the experts – it has all been said before and I could add nothing more. So tag along with me to find out what angling is really all about, and along the way I hope it will spark an interest with people who have not experienced this wonderful sport and resonate with those who have.

Yours (and tight lines)
Mike Fox

CHAPTER 1

The Brook

As a seven-year-old boy walking through the Shimming's Valley from Barton Lane in Petworth, Sussex, one afternoon in the summer holidays, I peered over the stone wall of a narrow-arched bridge into the clear waters of the meandering brook below. My reflection shimmered in the ripples of the water as it flowed around some large stones that broke through the surface. Under the bridge it was only a few inches deep, but the bed of the brook sloped off into deeper pools as it widened out downstream.

Under the overhanging branches of an old oak tree, a series of stepping stones had been randomly placed, crossing the brook from bank to bank. A short distance from these stones, on a wide bend, I spotted an older lad perched on a wicker basket on the edge of the bank and holding a fishing rod. I watched him with great interest. He was regularly swinging in small fish on the end of his line, unhooking them and then dropping them into a long net that was stretched over the edge of the bank and out into the water, secured by a stick at his feet.

I was intrigued by what he was doing and wandered down the bank to ask what he was catching. He grinned, and said proudly, "minnows". They were only two or three inches long, but to me they looked huge. He swung another into his open hand and showed me before unhooking it and placing it in his net.

I asked, "What do you do with them all?" and he replied, "I let them go when I've caught enough". I was fascinated and couldn't stop asking questions. I asked him about the bait he was using, the gear he had and where he had got it all from. The fisherman, who was only a few years older than me, answered with enthusiasm and didn't seem to mind my persistent inquisition.

After a while I left him alone and walked back along the stream towards the bridge. Pausing at the stepping stones, I sat on the largest one nearest to the bank and peered into the water once again. I noticed a movement and saw something on the bottom which looked like a fish, but it wasn't the same as the ones the fisherman was catching. It was mottled brown in colour and had a small body and a large, flattish head. No sooner had I seen it than it saw me and disappeared under another large stone. I lifted the stone and it swam away at great speed and was gone.

Underneath the stone I had just picked up were several creepy-crawly insects wriggling about. Some looked similar to the prawns you could buy from the fish shop, only a different colour and much smaller. There were also little hollow sticks about an inch long attached to the underside of the stone. One had a small head poking out from one end. I poked it with my finger and it broke in half, and inside was a maggot thing that looked not unlike those the fisherman was using to catch the minnows, but it had a black head with little legs behind and a whitish body. There were some other horrible-looking creepy crawlies that I didn't want to touch, which fell off back into the water. Intrigued by what I had discovered, I eventually put the stone back where I had taken it from and walked home.

I remember going home that afternoon, my head spinning with excitement, wishing I could do the same thing as the fisherman was doing. I couldn't wait to tell my mum and dad of my new-found interest and what I wanted to do during the holidays.

The next day couldn't come quick enough, and as soon as I could after breakfast I went back down to the brook. My home was only a few hundred yards away and it only took minutes to be on the banks again. Disappointingly the fisherman was not there, so I just sat on the bank all alone, once again gazing into the water. I had my wellies on this time and paddled into the shallower parts, walking upstream to where the water was coming from. I had to work my way around the deep parts by clinging onto the bank grasses and reeds, trying to prevent my wellies from sinking too far down into the soft mud.

Under the bridge I ventured where it was darker and cooler, having to bend right over to get underneath. "Boo!" I shrieked, just to listen to my echo bouncing off the arched brick sides of the bridge. Gingerly clinging on to the damp, slippery sides, I picked my way through to the other side and saw a length of barbed wire straddling the banks close to the water with bits of dead weed and rubbish trailing down onto the surface. I climbed over it, pushing the dangling branches of the overhanging trees to one side. Even though it was summer and quite warm out in the open sunshine, here it was dark and spooky, with very little bankside vegetation growing where the sun couldn't penetrate the trees.

I picked up stones from the bottom of the brook as I walked, but found fewer and fewer of the little grubs and crawly things. A bit further on an old tree had fallen from the bankside and was lying across the brook. It looked as though it had been there for many years and it was covered in damp moss with toadstools growing out from its uprooted base. I sat with my legs astride the fallen tree trunk for a while, just looking around, and noticed that the water began to get a little deeper on the other side. I sat for a while longer, watching and listening to the birds singing and the leaves on the trees rustling in the wind. Patiently I waited, I don't know what for.

Then something happened which startled me so much that I scrambled off the tree and out of the water as quickly as I could. I saw a huge black snake-like thing swimming towards me up the brook from where I had been walking. It seemed to be as long and as fat as my right arm. I could see its mouth opening and closing, and its eyes appeared to be fixed on me.

I began shaking with fear and clung to a tree on the relative safety of the bank. I knew what this was – an eel. I had heard that they would eat anything they could find that was edible, and I imagined that included me. I didn't hang around much longer, but ran off into the warm sunshine of the open fields, up the hill and home for my dinner.

That evening I told my dad what I had seen and he laughed, reassuring me that an eel wouldn't eat me, and that I should try to catch it. He told me people in the East End of London ate eels in jelly, and that if I caught it I should kill it and we could eat it. I really didn't fancy eating it. I did want to catch it, but how was I going to do that? I didn't have the equipment the fisherman had, and I didn't have any money to buy a fishing rod and reel. But that wasn't going to stop me. With a lot of imagination and a little help and encouragement from my dad I set myself up and made my own very first fishing rod.

It consisted of the longest bean cane I could find from my dad's allotment, net curtain wire eyes, string and a thin bent nail. I screwed the curtain eyes into the cane and threaded the string through the eyes to the thickest end of the cane, where I tied the string to the last eye. I didn't have a reel, but it looked the part anyway. Using my Cub Scout skills to tie knots (a granny knot), I tied the bent nail to the other end of the string, and I was all ready for my very first fishing expedition. For bait, I could pick up worms from under rocks and leaves I found on my way down Barton Lane, putting them into a jam jar for safe keeping. Dad told me they would work.

The next day, I couldn't get to the brook fast enough. I collected half a dozen big fat juicy worms on the way – it would be easy to slide these up the nail and over the chunky knot. I was so excited.

Overcoming my fear of eels remarkably quickly, I returned to the fallen tree where I had seen that massive snake-like thing. It was of course nowhere to be seen. Once again I straddled myself across the tree. Then I baited the nail with a worm and dangled it over into the deepest area of the brook I could reach to. I sat and I sat and I sat, for what seemed like an eternity, although it was probably less than an hour. I had no perception of time at that age, but what is time when you are only seven? I hadn't seen anything resembling a fish or and eel, but I wasn't too bothered and it didn't deter me from trying other areas around the tree.

I gave up trying after a while and ventured a little further up the brook beside another fallen tree stump that lay submerged along the nearside edge. Impaling another worm on my bent nail I dropped it down into the water close to the tree. I waited for a short time, watching the worm wriggling on the bottom of the brook in the clear water. A nervous feeling of trepidation came over me as I waited for something to happen.

And then, suddenly, it did. An eel appeared from nowhere, then slowly moved toward the worm and sucked it in; it even swallowed the nail. My heart must have missed several beats. I yanked my rod into the air as hard as I could and the eel came with it, shooting out of the water at what seemed to be a hundred miles an hour. It landed just behind me, still attached to the string. Finally letting go of the worm and nail, it wriggled off into the dead leaves and twigs that littered the bank, eventually falling back into the water.

I stood there shaking like a leaf with excitement. The elation was beyond anything I had experienced before. Even though the eel was smaller than the one I had seen the previous day, I was jubilant that I had caught it; well sort of, it had only just got away. Shaking from head to toe, with sheer joy this time instead of fear, I ran home to tell mum and dad of my achievements.

After that it made no odds to me what the weather was like; every day I would be itching to get back to the brook and explore more of it. Through field and marshland, under and over bridges I would trek, sometimes staying away for several hours before doing my best to remember to go home for lunch or tea. Occasionally I would be late and get a bit of a telling off from mum and dad, but secretly it didn't trouble me, as I was getting used to it.

The success of my first adventure spurred me on for many days to try to catch more eels from other areas of the brook. I did manage to get a couple onto the bank, but more often than not the nail would pull from the eel's mouth, leaving it to disappear panic-stricken back into the freshly-disturbed murky depths. I gave that method up after a while as it didn't work as well as I had hoped, and concentrated on the other species that inhabited the water.

Not having a proper fishing rod at the time, I would paddle in my wellington boots in the shallow pools learning how to find those little fish with flat heads, and soon found that they were called bullheads. I learned to catch them by creeping up behind them and cupping my hands together, then slowly sliding my hands into the water and quickly clasping my fingers around them. I could catch three or four in a session, but more managed to escape than I caught. The fun part was in the stealth of lifting the stones and then pouncing before they realised something wasn't as it should be. I soon learned that the best conditions for catching were dull cloudy days rather than bright sunny ones. I didn't think they could see me as easily on cloudy days as I didn't cast so much of a shadow.

Once caught, I would put them into a jam-jar of water and watch them swim around. They were funny-looking things with sharply-tapered bodies and two large wing-like fins behind the head and they didn't look like proper fish at all to me, but I found them fascinating nonetheless. I always put them back after a while to swim away, believing that I could catch them again another day.

I would repeat these expeditions at every opportunity available to me, after school, during the school holidays and at weekends. I would explore the brook all the way up to the Horsham Road, where it became nothing more than a shallow ditch with a narrow trickle of water. This was the Hampers Green end, and I didn't go any further because of the troublesome reputation this estate had – I was told not to play with the Hampers Green boys. North Mead, the bit in the middle, was OK though. Occasionally I would meet up with Martin, a school friend who lived there, and we would both go down to the brook and do some fishing, but Martin wasn't as enthusiastic as me and I always ended up much wetter and more splattered in mud when I was with him than when on my own. We spent more time throwing rocks and bits of dead wood into the water to see who could produce the biggest splash and get the other one the wettest. But it was all great fun and always in good humour and we never fell out over a good soaking. One time Martin fell into a bed of stinging nettles and he wasn't very happy, but I laughed my socks off, which didn't go down too well at all.

It wasn't long before he got the last laugh though. One day we were walking towards a stretch of the brook we wanted to fish, but couldn't get to it from our side because there were too many trees and bushes. The only access was on the other side of the brook, through a field and across a large bog. As we approached the bog the ground began to get wetter and softer. My discerning friend announced he would go first and I should put my feet in the same places as his as we moved across the marshland. There were clumps of grass with firm root systems within stepping distance of each other, which made the going quite easy at first, but then they too became wetter and softer. Instinctively we increased our speed, thinking that if we went faster, less weight would be put onto these clumps of grass. It turned out not to be the cleverest idea in the world. Martin managed to hop to the safety of dry land, leaving me behind. My right foot slipped off one of the grass clumps, plunging me into the cold, wet bog with a distressing gloop. I sank right up to my thigh, and my left leg was at 90 degrees to the right with my wellie slowly filling with cold, muddy water, and I was stuck fast, not being able to move at all. I didn't know whether to laugh or cry.

I began to panic, thinking I was doomed and would be swallowed up by the bog and drown. Naturally Martin found this totally hilarious – I couldn't make out if he was soaking wet from his efforts to get to dry land or whether he was wetting himself with laughter. Eventually, being the Scouts that we were, we managed to get me out using fallen tree branches as a makeshift pulley system. My relief at getting out alive soon turned to frustration as I realised that my right welly boot was somewhere down in the depths of the now stinking bog.

Deciding that we couldn't continue our expedition smelling like fresh farmyard slurry and me with one boot, we decided to go home. But how were we going to get back across the bog? Martin had a brilliant idea. "We could always walk around the bog instead of going through it," he said...

We squelching our way back home, totally plastered in mud yet again, and mum was understandably not terribly amused. She sighed, "Oh no, not again! Take those trousers off outside."

One other event will always stick in my memory. Every summer the last field before the Horsham road magically turned into a cornfield. For most of the year it was just like a desert, with clumps of grass sprouting from the old ruts and clumps of soil left behind by the previous year's harvesting. I could always take a short cut directly across the field to the stream when it was in this condition, but when the field was freshly ploughed and the new crop was being sown, I had to walk around the outside, as I was always told to. But in the height of summer, when the corn was growing, the trek around the perimeter of the field was worth every extra step. I would see fieldmice scurrying from the surrounding grass banks into the corn and emerge again with their mouths full of fresh seed. Skylarks soared high in to the sky. I would hear them at first, then peer into the bright blue sky with eyes squinting in the sunshine, trying to spot them. It was always very difficult to see them to begin with, but eventually my eyes would focus and there they were, tiny dark silhouettes fluttering in an infinity of open space.

Sometimes at the end of the summer, I was lucky enough to see the corn being harvested, and when it had been cut, a huge flock of lapwings would converge in the middle of the field, picking off any edible morsels left behind by the combine harvester. It was a magical time of year to be out and about with so much activity going on in the countryside. A buzzard occasionally perched itself on the top bough of a dead oak tree that had been struck by lightning many years ago. I didn't see any field mice around when he was about, or any other little animals, as even the rabbits, of which there were many, scampered off to hide in their burrows beneath the hedgerows.

This was a long time ago and my recollection of exact timescales has become somewhat jaded, but my memories of this and many other adventures at the brook will remain with me for the rest of my life.

CHAPTER 2

The Stream

In the summer of 1966 my family moved from our old cottage in North Street to the quieter side of town. I was nearly eight now and didn't share their excitement at moving into a newly-built detached house with a large garden at the so called 'posh' end of town. I remember sitting in the front of a friend's cattle transporter saying goodbye to Priest Cottages, saddened at the thought of leaving the only home I had known. All our furniture and belongings were piled high in the back of this dilapidated old truck. Fortunately it had been cleaned out of poo and straw, but it still smelt like a farmyard though and the cab floor was smeared with squashed cigarette butts and dried mud – at least I assumed it was mud. Bits of paper, sweet wrappers and cigarette packets littered the dashboard. I expect our friend didn't charge my dad very much for his services. There weren't any removal firms in Petworth in those days and the nearest one would have been expensive.

Our new home was in Sheepdown Close, originally named Mount Pleasant. It was all very nice, with the bowling club and lawn tennis club right at the end of the garden. Everyone there spoke with exaggerated gentility and all sounded extremely polite. This was not really my cup of tea, as I had no interest in playing bowls or tennis. My immediate concerns lay at the foot of the Sheepdowns, not half a mile from my new home. I knew it as the Brook, but for some reason the people here called it the stream. I suppose "stream" sounds posher than "brook".

This was the middle part, and it began at the bridge on the A283, which we called the Brighton road. The stream was a little bit wider than the brook, deeper with slower-moving water, and one part had an island in the middle. I needed a proper fishing rod to fish here, but there were more trees and brambles covering the banks, which made it much more difficult to get down to the water.

As I walked along the banks one day, I saw circular ripples appearing from nowhere on the surface of the water. They grew wider as they moved out towards the banks. If I looked very closely, occasionally I would see a little fish come up and then quickly turn away and go back down to the bottom. They looked like the same type of fish the fisherman was catching from the Brook at Shimming's last summer.

This discovery really excited me, and the desire to own a fishing rod was growing much stronger. Now I really, really wanted one.

A little further down, a wooden footbridge crossed the stream at the Virgin Mary Springs, connecting the public footpath from Byworth to Petworth. The water that fell from a short exposed section of pipe into a little pool was always cold, crystal clear and perfectly drinkable. It was very refreshing on a hot summer's day. The never-ending trickle of the fresh spring water found its way under the footpath into the stream through another pipe.

I felt much more grown up here, as this was the place where the bigger boys hung out. The "bigger boys" came from the Herbert Shiner School and several times a group of them ran past me along the footpath in their PE gear. I would soon learn in years to come that this was the cross-country running route that almost everyone at secondary school dreaded. But I was still at primary school and didn't have to do this kind of stuff yet, so I was unperturbed.

The top rail of the wooden bridge was a perfect height for me to lean over and watch for fish moving about in the clear water below. Just upstream of the bridge there was a long winding right-hand bend where the gentle breeze created a constant motion of light ripples, endlessly creeping down towards me with the current. It was quite deep, and it was impossible to see the bottom of the stream in the reflection of the sky on the surface. I could only gaze and wonder, and spent ages watching fish coming up to feed under the surface.

Swarms of tiny little midges were dancing around in spheres, forming a translucent haze just above the surface. Round and round they would go; sometimes one would rest on the water, and then a fish would rise from the depths and take it. There was so much going on here beside the stream, and it lured me into a dream world where time was of no significance, although in reality, I suppose it went by in a flash.

The daydreaming wasn't the only thing that flashed by, as a kingfisher lived somewhere nearby. It would often zoom past me, up and down the middle of the stream in a flash of blue, so fast I couldn't see it in any detail. I never did find its nest, but it couldn't have been far away as almost every time I was there I saw it flying through the valley – or perhaps there were two, or maybe a whole family somewhere.

Squirrels lived in large numbers high up in the towering fir trees. In autumn they would often come down to the hazel tree which stood beside the bridge to harvest the nuts and then scamper back to their homes. Ducks and other waterfowl would fight in the boggy pond that appeared in a dip of the adjacent field after a long spell of rain. It would dry up in the summer, but it was a hot spot for finding frogs and toads hiding under stones or in amongst thick clumps of grass. There were rabbits everywhere, especially in the early mornings, and if I was lucky, sometimes I would see through the trees a family of roe deer feeding at the top of the hill. I recall one of the prettiest sights that caught my attention were the yellowhammers hopping and fluttering around the prickly branches of the gorse bushes that spread across much of the hillside.

I found the funniest and most entertaining animals of the Sheepdowns were the herd of goats that roamed freely in the fields. The little ones were very timid and stayed close to the nanny, but the billy goat looked quite scary and I always made sure I kept well away from him. Rather than have an argument with this huge, handsome and very protective billy goat, I would walk around the outside of the field to get to the stream. I thought this to be the more favourable option than walking down the trodden footpath through the middle of the field and get a pair of over-sized goat horns slammed against my rear end.

The stream followed a route at the foot of the Sheepdowns through what everyone called Bluebell Wood and into open fields, eventually reaching the bridge at the Waterworks Station in Haslingbourne Lane. I was told there were lots of trout in these parts and there was an area of the stream fenced off with no public right of way. It had two lengths of chicken wire fencing stretched across the stream about a hundred yards apart. The local pig farmer owned this stretch, and it was at the bottom of the garden of his farmhouse, which was on the other side of the stream. I understood he kept brown trout in there for the family table. I knew not to cross this fence through fear of being shot at. Local gossip rumoured that the farmer was very protective of this bit of stream and he had a reputation for chasing people off his land armed with a 12-bore shotgun. I'm not sure if it was true, but I didn't fancy finding out for myself by getting peppered with gunshot.

The stream ran past the waterworks, becoming deeper and even wider, and it was possible to see a few trout in these parts. There was no footpath here and not many people walked down by the stream, so I suppose the fish weren't bothered so much by dogs jumping in and disturbing them, as often happened further up. I was able to get quite close to these fish before they saw me and then disappear under the trees on the opposite side. Somewhere (quite possibly in a volume of Arthur Mee's Children's Encyclopaedia) I had found out about the art of tickling fish and how to do it, and I wondered if it really worked and if I could actually master this skill. The trout here would sit just under the nearside bank grasses in the shallower water, and I thought that if I crept up behind them I would be able to touch them. I attempted this several times by crawling along the ground on my belly, leaning over the edge of the bank, sliding my arm into the water and slowly moving towards the trout. The closest I ever got was to touch their tails before they would bolt off up-stream and out of sight. I clearly couldn't master this ancient art of fish tickling and all I got for my efforts were wet, freezing cold arms and of course I was plastered in mud. I didn't take that kind of fishing any further and haven't tried it again to this day. I was sure it would be much easier with a rod and line.

As Christmas of 1968 drew closer, I was hoping above all that I would get the fishing rod I had been dreaming of. I had made enough noise about it over the past months, so surely the penny would have dropped and Santa would oblige this year.

Finally Christmas Day arrived and the presents were there on Christmas morning under the tree as they always were, and there it was. I couldn't see through the wrapping, but I knew by the shape. Cruelly, mum and dad said I was to open this present after all the rest had been opened and a note of who sent them had been written down. I always had to write to the people who sent me the presents, thanking them for their generosity and thoughtfulness and let them know how very much I would enjoy playing with my new gifts.

One of the presents I received was a large hardback book entitled *Fish & Fishing*. It had everything in it, with drawings on how to set up a fishing rod and tackle and instruction on how to use all kinds of other fishing gear. It had descriptions of all the fish you could find in British waters and what they eat. It contained everything I could want to learn about fishing in full colour, and would be my fishing bible for many years.

Finally the time came for me to open the last present, which just happened to be from mum and dad, and it didn't take me long to unwrap it. There it was, laid out on the floor before me, packed in clear plastic on a strip of cardboard with a reel separately wrapped in plastic at one end. It was a two-piece, 6ft, white glass fibre rod with red thread fixing the line guides at intervals all the way from the tip down to a black plastic handle. The reel was an Intrepid Black Prince fixed spool, with a separate spool of nylon fishing line just begging to be wound around the reel spool. A pack of proper hooks, a couple of weird-shaped floats with small rubber rings and weights of many different sizes were included in the pack.

I was uncontrollably excited and couldn't wait to set it all up and use it. It was December, it was blooming cold and everywhere was frozen, but it didn't matter, I had my first-ever set of proper fishing gear and I was just a little bit happier than I had ever been before.

My immediate thought was that I could practise casting in the back garden and could put a washing up bowl at the far end of the grass as a target to try and land the float into. It was the best idea ever, and after a while I got quite good at casting – I was at least hitting the bowl with every cast, even if it didn't go in every time. I spent hours repeating this practice in all weathers – it didn't bother me at all. Rain, sleet or snow, I was there casting away until my arms got so tired they ached.

At last mum and dad were realising my insatiable interest with the outdoors, and especially with fishing, but unfortunately for me they knew nothing about it, and nor did any other member of my family. My mum's side of the family came from Brighton and the only fishing they did was sea fishing off the pier or from the beach, which is not quite the same, and in any case I was less interested in sea fishing. However, Brighton did have an excellent aquarium close to the sea front which housed all kinds of species, including freshwater fish. As most of my family still lived in Brighton, we would regularly visit them on a Sunday. I forget how many times I managed to persuade dad to take me to the aquarium, but over the period of a few years it was quite a few. I remember that one of the best visits was when the fish had just been fed. I was fixated by the behaviour of the fish, and I must have spent hours leaning up against the tanks staring into their aquatic homes watching how they fed. Some species fed up near the surface, some in the middle and others at the bottom. I obsessively absorbed every new experience involving fish and fishing, most importantly learning new things all the time.

It wasn't until well into the new year of 1969 that I could use my new fishing gear on the water for the first time. It was probably a Saturday morning when I went to the stream armed with my shiny new rod and reel, a couple of slices of bread and a large glass jar with string tied around the rim for a handle. On my way down to the stream I would lift rocks to find small redworms and slugs and put them in a tin to use for bait in addition to the bread. It was all in the book about what and where I should look to find natural bait to catch fish. The book also told me about those maggots with black heads and legs that lived in those little stick things I found under stones in the brook all that time ago. I would collect lots of those and use them for bait as well. I called them "stick maggots", but the book called them "caddis fly larvae".

I would fish the slower, deeper pools of the stream where there was somewhere comfortable I could find to sit down on the bank. Using the bait I had found and the bread I made into a paste, which I also learned how to make from the book, I made my first casts, and you can only imagine the excitement that ran through my body when the float bobbed and I would strike to find a minnow attached to my hook. It was a huge leap forward for me as now I was a proper fisherman, just like the older boy I met at the brook.

I remember taking my catch of several minnows home in the glass jar to show mum and dad. When I got home I filled an old tin bath with tap water and tipped the minnows into it. I also put some rocks, soil and grass in as well to make it a little more like home for them. Unfortunately the minnows didn't last very long and they died. I felt so sad. I didn't know why they had died at the time, but after that I never brought my catch home again. And catch I did, many times over, but only the minnows, and as the months went by I soon grew bored with fishing the stream. I needed to experience another challenge.

CHAPTER 3

From Crawfold Farm to the Rother

Growing up in the country was a privilege I didn't appreciate at the time; I just took it for granted that this was the normal way of life. I was always out and about, either on my own, with mates or with the family. Local trips in the car on a Sunday afternoon to other parts of West Sussex was a regular event for our family. It didn't have to be far, and sometimes it was only four or five miles.

For many of these outings the family would drive over to Crawfold Farm near the village of Balls Cross on the way to Kirdford. In the springtime we would drive to a small wood somewhere on the farm to pick wild daffodils. These flowers blanketed the ground and there were millions of them, stretching as far as the eye could see. Other people would join in with the harvest and like us, leave with baskets full to the brim. Mum would decorate the local church with them in preparation for the Easter festival.

My brother and I always looked forward to these trips, as dad would allow us to get out of the car and ride the rear bumper as he drove along the field track. Mum would be petrified about us falling off and often pleaded with dad to slow down in case we came a cropper, but we never did. It seemed we were travelling quite fast, but in reality we were only going about four miles an hour. Nevertheless it was great fun.

Close friends of the family managed Crawfold Farm, and they would quite often invite us over for tea. I found that quite boring, but some of the time I would muck about with one of their sons on the farm, which was great fun. Much of the farm was out of bounds to us kids because of the machinery, but we would play on the straw bales in the barn and go rat catching, with the aim of beating the blighters to death with fence posts. Most of them got away, but we did get one or two and had plenty of laughs falling arse upwards over the bales while chasing them around.

Like most farms, Crawfold had a pond – in fact two. One was the goldfish pond and home to some huge golden orfe and shubunkins, and family rules clearly stated that fishing was forbidden. The main pond, on the other hand, contained lots of roach, rudd, perch, carp and eels, and it was only a short walk from the yard. When the weather was good Richard and I would spend a couple of hours fishing while the adults nattered in the house. On summer days during the school holidays dad would drive me over to the farm before he went to work, so I could spend the day fishing, and then collect me again after work. I would have a packed lunch and a bottle of squash to keep me going through the day. Occasionally the farm managers, Aunty Tess or Uncle Jack would come down to the pond to check that I was all right and hadn't fallen in. Aunty Tess and Uncle Jack weren't really my uncle and aunty, but as they were good friends of the family, that was how I was brought up to call them.

By this time I was buying maggots from the butcher's shop in town. I could buy a quarter of a pint of fresh white maggots for sixpence. They were kept in sawdust and always had a small piece of old meat gristle in with them to keep them fed. It felt quite normal to go into a butcher's and come out with a bag of maggots – all the fishermen did it. Somehow I don't think it would be allowed these days!

I would sit for hours on a sandy bank under a big oak tree casting out towards the bushes on the far bank. There were many other places to fish on this pond, but I liked the comfort of the sandy bank and the cosiness of being under the tree, which provided much-needed shade during those hot summer days.

After several visits to the pond I soon learned that the mornings were always best for catching fish. I never caught a carp, but I would always catch plenty of roach and rudd and the occasional eel. My enthusiasm dwindled somewhat after I'd caught a few eels, because they would always wrap themselves around the line, swallow the hook and generally make a right mess of my tackle with their stinking slime, and I would nearly always have to take it apart and set it all up again. So I was glad that there weren't too many in the pond.

I would usually catch several fish in the morning, but by lunchtime the fish didn't seem to feed as much and I wouldn't get any bites for quite a while. This was a good thing, because it gave me time to have a sandwich and a packet of crisps. It didn't bother me that my fingers were sticky with fish slime, sawdust under my fingernails from the maggots and seriously stinking of ammonia. It was all part of being out fishing, and probably enhanced the taste of my boring old ham sandwiches, which were sometimes curled at the edges.

I found that generally in the afternoons and especially on the bright sunny days, the fish were not so interested in feeding, and my thinking at that time was they must have all gone somewhere for an afternoon nap. I would get a little bored when the bites stopped coming and found myself alternative entertainment by staging maggot races in the tray of my tackle box. Two maggots would be placed side by side and set free at one end to wriggle away to the other, and the winner would have the luxury of being returned to the maggot box to live a while longer, while the loser would be put on the hook to drown, or at best get eaten by a fish.

This short-term loss of angling concentration quickly passed and renewed expectation of catching more fish would overcome my boredom. I would then try another part of the pond for a while, usually without success, and the boredom returned. The many different varieties of geese and ducks would entertain me for a while as they waddled down to the pond in one long regimental line, probably in order of hierarchy. They would paddle a full circuit around the pond and then waddle back to where they came from in the field.

When the boredom really set in, I wouldn't wait for dad to come and collect me at the end of the afternoon – I would pack my gear away and walk home. It was about four miles back to Petworth by the road and a little shorter through the fields and along the farm tracks. I knew I wouldn't see anybody going that way, but if I walked along the road, sometimes someone who knew me would drive by and stop to give me a lift home, so it was always the better option.

The book had taught me that fishing was nearly always better in the mornings and then later in the evenings, and for me this proved to be the case many times over. Sometimes I would fish in the evenings for a couple of hours while mum and dad visited AT and UJ in the farm house and I would catch plenty of fish during these times. As I got older and a little more experienced, I found my angling knowledge was improving each time I went fishing and realised the weather conditions played a huge part in how many fish I caught. I was told that fish would feed better when it was raining because they thought anglers wouldn't turn out in bad weather. I honestly believed this for quite a while, but I soon learned that the real reason for this was more to do with the light factor.

I think I must have been about 12 years old when I was given another book about fishing by a family friend who lived close to the River Rother at Coultershaw Mill, just to the south of Petworth. The book was called *Mr Crabtree Goes Fishing*. It was mostly about river fishing, with the fictional characters of Mr Crabtree and his son Peter, and was more of an instructional guide with detailed sketches. Whilst reading the text and looking at the pictures I would imagine myself to be in the story, fishing alongside them, it was that engaging. I learned so much from this book and I must have read it from cover to cover, time and time again.

When I was asked what I would like for Christmas and birthdays I would always ask for more fishing equipment or books. A favourite present of mine was a wicker fishing basket that could be used as a seat and a storage box in which I could put all my gear. The only problem was that it used to squeak like mad when it was sat on and I always wondered if the fish could hear it when I fidgeted or got my things out of it at the water's edge. I was also given a landing net and a pole to land my fish, and also a much longer keepnet to keep them in during my day's fishing. A set of weighing scales, bank sticks, more floats, hooks and split shot and all sorts of other fishing-related bits and bobs soon amassed in my bright orange plastic cantilever screw and nail box, which made an ideal tackle box. Pegley Davies was the brand name of the majority of my tackle, as it was sold in the local tackle shop, which was really an electrical appliance shop which dedicated a section to fishing tackle, mainly I think because the owners of the shop were keen anglers themselves.

What sticks in my mind mostly about Pegley Davies was the hooks to nylon sold in card wallets and individually stored in transparent sleeves. A brilliant invention, I thought, which made tying on a hook so much easier and eliminated the unsightly granny knot at the eye of the hook which inevitably made the bait appear less natural.

I was learning fast, and the desire to fish rivers became

my next ambition. I had a couple of school friends who were also keen on fishing and had talked about trying the River Rother at Coultershaw Mill and further down to the junction of the old canal and on to Shopham Bridge. I knew where the mill was, but I hadn't a clue about the canal or Shopham Bridge. I didn't even know Petworth had a canal at that time!

One of my schoolmates would sometimes bring into class a copy of his dad's *Angling Times* for us all to read. It had pages full of stories of fishermen's catches, with pictures of them holding big fish or bulging keep nets of roach and bream. We would go giddy with excitement, just wishing that this could be us one day sharing our own stories of our adventures with the world. None of our fishing trips came close to those we read about in the *Angling Times*, but our desire to emulate their successes was boundless. We could only dream.

My schoolmates had recently joined Petworth Angling Club with their dads and said I would need to do so if I wanted to fish the river, as only club members were allowed. Fortunately my dad knew the club secretary, so after much badgering I became the latest recruit to the junior section. I was so proud of my new membership card and rule book that I took it everywhere with me (except school) and read through it many times over, memorising the club rules so I wouldn't get in to trouble by unwittingly doing something illegal. The booklet had sketch maps of the river Rother and ponds that I never knew existed and showed you where all the access points were. It also had a list of species I could expect to catch in the different waters that were owned by the club. dace, chub, grayling, perch, carp, barbel and pike were all species I had never caught before. It was all very exciting.

Before I was allowed to go to the river alone, dad said I needed a bit more experience and I would need to go fishing with somebody who knew what they were doing. No sooner said than done. I was taken to the Chichester Canal by the owner of the fishing tackle shop in Petworth. He and a friend were having a day's fishing on the canal and asked dad if I would like to go with them. Would I? Not half! It would be my first time out fishing with a proper angler.

The morning of the fishing trip arrived and I was taken to the A27 road bridge to the south of Chichester where the canal went underneath. I was so excited that I couldn't stop chattering about fishing during the journey and must have driven my new friends bonkers before we had even begun to fish.

The canal began at Chichester Basin, near the city centre, passing through Hunston and on towards the yacht marina, ending at Chichester Harbour. The canal was not navigable at that time because of the weed, but there were several long stretches that were accessible and perfect for anglers. The water was very clear and it was possible to see fish swimming amongst the weed.

As we walked along the towpath my friend spotted a small shoal of perch in a clearing out in the middle of the canal. He told me to set myself up there and have a go at them, and he and his mate would fish nearer the bridge. I honestly think they wanted me as far away from them as possible, without being totally out of their sight, but I didn't care. I did as I was told, as quickly as I could, all fingers and thumbs, all the time glancing out at the shoal of perch, and excitedly cast out.

My large swan quill float landed straight in the middle of the shoal and spooked the lot. They all disappeared out of sight instantly and I never saw them again. I was really pleased with my accurate cast, but it was another lesson learned; never cast into the middle of a shoal of fish. Always cast past or to the side and drag the float back slowly over them. I wish I had been told that beforehand. It was probably in the book, but I must have forgotten. Any way I managed to catch a few roach after that and went home quite happy with a few tales to tell mum and dad.

That was to be the one and only time I fished the Chichester Canal, as my sights were now clearly set on fishing the river. My problem was that the 6ft glass fibre rod I had so dearly loved when I was first given it was far too short for river fishing. I needed something at least twice as long.

I managed to scrape together some pocket money from working in my dad's shop on a Saturday morning; the usual stuff like sweeping up, washing the windows, cleaning out the rubbish pit and generally fetching and carrying. I would be paid 50p for a morning's work, eventually rising to £1 after much creeping and crawling (begging) to the boss. It took a few months, but with Christmas and birthday money I soon had enough put together to go out and buy a new rod and reel. It was a 13-foot hollow cane float road made by Rodrill of London. The reel was an Abu Garcia closed face with a push button to release the line, and was at the cutting edge of technology at the time. Well, that's what I was told!

It was like starting all over again with casting, and I

certainly needed some instruction on how to use my new gear. Our old friend Peter Carter from Coultershaw took me to the mill pool one day and showed me how it was done, and soon I was trotting the line down the current like a pro. It was fantastic. I don't remember catching anything on my first outing, but after that I was allowed to go to the mill on my own. Initially I would walk the mile and a half there and back again, but I soon got tired of that, so I figured out a way of carrying my gear on my bike. It was awkward and probably unsafe, but in those days who cared about health and safety? I was going fishing, and nothing and no one was going to stop me.

In the beginning I remember only catching a few gudgeon and a tiny "bootlace" of an eel. It was probably no more than six inches long, but I shall never forget it. I suppose some people would have given up after days of not catching many fish or even one large one, but not me. I was just as hopeful and just as eager to return to the river as the first day I went.

I was now in my teens and going to grammar school at Midhurst. As luck would have it, the school playing fields sloped off at one side, reaching right down to the River Rother at the Old Mill on the Easebourne Road. The location couldn't get any better, and it isn't any wonder that my school reports often read "Michael seems to be more interested in what is going on outside the classroom than in". OK then clever teacher, don't sit me by the window! Not exactly rocket science, is it? But sit by the window I did, all the way through my schooling years, and I suppose you could say that is probably why I was never even close to being top of the class in most subjects. I was good at Biology and Rural Studies though.

Out of school, I was back on the river at Petworth as often as I could, learning about the changing currents, whirlpools and back eddies caused by the water coming through the mill wheel from the river above which is the making of Coultershaw Millpool.

Fish would rest up just off the turbulence of these waters in the slack areas, but finding them wasn't as easy as it would seem. Most days I would only catch a few dace and gudgeon, but on one occasion I found a shoal of bream and caught four of them, each weighing 3lb or thereabouts. My cheaper-than-cheap scales were not that accurate and only went up in ¼ lb markings to a maximum of 25lb, but they were close enough, and to be honest the weight of my fish didn't bother me then and still doesn't now to be honest. I have always thought younger and smaller fish are much prettier than their older, bigger and more battle-scarred relatives. That isn't to say I don't enjoy catching bigger fish; I do, but I never set out to be a specimen hunter and never shall.

A little further downstream from the mill through a forest of scrub, nettles and reeds, some taller than me, was a fork in the river where a side stream entered the main flow, creating a deeper channel where fish would lie in wait for food coming down the converging currents. It was here that I caught my first chub, on a worm. Not a huge one, only about 2lb, but it was my first and certainly my most memorable, as it took me ages to land while it fought against the confused currents. This swim also held a good head of dace, and I spent many an hour catching these beautiful little bars of silver.

Out in the open field, the "cattle drink" was another swim where dace and grayling lurked over the far side under overhanging trees in an area of faster current. It was here I caught my first grayling. It was probably the proudest moment of my early years of being an angler, as the grayling was a prized fish amongst most anglers, especially my schoolmates, who constantly talked about their fighting capabilities, their beauty and their huge colourful iridescent dorsal fins.

My angling career was really taking off, and I was still only about 14. I would venture off further down the river to the beginning of the old canal, but it was a long way to walk, especially if I had walked or cycled from home in the first instance. I didn't spend a great deal of time down these parts for that reason and would rather spend more time fishing at the mill stretch, although it was a very pleasant walk along the river bank, dodging the cowpats.

Now cowpats may not be the first choice for a topic of conversation, but they played a huge part in my angling days. I didn't always have a tub of maggots from the butchers to use as bait. In my early years as a piscator, I learned to be resourceful and find fishing bait of the more natural kind. It didn't take long for me to learn that cowpats were nature's larder for fresh grubs and worms. However, not all cowpats would contain such insects and bugs, so a careful process of selection was required. Fresh steaming ones were obviously a no-go area, as were those up to two days old. Usually the best would be about three days old as they had dried out on the surface, forming a hard outer crust, and were a little softer in the middle but not wet. Lifting the frisbee-sized pancake carefully, I would find dung worms and beetle grubs foraging around and collect them into a bait box. I found the little red worms were the most productive baits for dace and grayling. The little minnows were quite partial to them as well and the large white beetle grubs were excellent for chub.

Occasionally I would find little white maggots by the dozen, but these were too small to put on the hook and not worthwhile poking about in a pile of poo for. I had been told that wasp grubs were good for chub in the summer months, but there was no way I was attempting to gather any of those for love nor money, should I come across a wasps' nest.

Shopham Bridge was the other stretch of the river that I had yet to fish, but that was soon to become reality. Another friend and his brother, Richard (Dickie) and Michael (Mike) were also keen on fishing, and one day their mum took us to the river in her van and told us she would return to pick us up later that afternoon. I don't remember much about any fishing of that first particular day, due to the amount of frivolity and mucking about, so I don't think a lot of serious fishing actually took place. I think more time was spent pulling our lines from trees and bushes and generally untangling knots and loops from around the float and hook than actually fishing. It was just hilarious fun.

What I do remember is the joint exploration of the river and its little feeder streams, which would prove to be invaluable for future visits. An important feeder stream of this stretch was sourced from Burton Pond about three quarters of a mile (as the crow flies) to the west. It was only about six or seven feet wide and at most a couple of feet deep with its clear waters flowing over stones and rocks, absorbing oxygen on its way to the main river, where the bed of the stream turned to sand. In the summer months this area would be a nursery to young perch and gudgeon and there would be hundreds of them, all facing upstream feeding on tiny creatures brought down with the flow. I would throw a maggot in to the middle of the pulsating shoal as they held station in the current and several fish would rush to devour the maggot, but they would find it too big and play tug 'o' war with it until a slightly larger fish would intervene and eventually swallow the elongated and desiccated skin.

This little stream was home to an abundance of wildlife, from dragonflies to kingfishers and from water voles to grass snakes, but our quarry was the big chub that sheltered under the relative safety of a fallen tree bough on a bend. There were usually two fish of about 4lb but occasionally an even larger one, probably 5lb or more, would join them. This larger fish, we found, generally lived under the little footbridge a little further upstream and quite often migrated down to the main river to feed. It would certainly give me the run around as I tried time and time again to catch it from under the bridge, to no avail. I'm sure it could see me leaning over the side, as I could clearly see it swimming around in the gentle current.

I remember catching one of the smaller chub on a worm that I trundled along the bottom through the overhanging vegetation and under the fallen bough. It put up a dogged fight as I refused to give it line, which thankfully was strong enough and tied to a large enough hook. The adrenalin was pumping through my body while I was kneeling down reaching out with my landing net, temporarily unaware of being stung by nettles and scratched by thistles. The euphoria of catching such a beautiful fish far exceeded the realisation of the annoying tingling pain from every exposed area of my skin until the fish was returned and I had calmed down from the excitement.

On another occasion the three of us returned to this part of the river and Mike and I were fishing either side of the stream estuary while Dickie persevered for the big chub under the tree. Mike and I were happily catching small dace, perch and gudgeon when the most bloodcurdling scream bellowed from beneath trees of the stream. Mike and I jumped to our feet to see what on earth was going on, finding Dickie hanging on to his bent double fishing rod, prizing a huge chub from out under the fallen tree bough. Shaking with laughter and enthusiasm for Dickie, Mike somehow netted the fish after stern instruction from Dickie and heaved it up on to the bank. We were all jumping about with excitement, just as much as the fish was jumping about with disdain of being wrenched from its watery sanctuary. The grin on Dickie's face was from ear to ear in triumphant admiration of this beautiful creature as he reluctantly, but proudly, returned it to the stream. We had no idea of its weight, but to this day it is possibly the biggest chub I have ever seen.

The excitement of the stream was short-lived unfortunately. On returning visits, spread over a couple of seasons, it was obvious the chub had moved on, and they never returned. The dace remained for a little while longer as did the perch and gudgeon. But every autumn of each year the perch and gudgeon also disappeared, and I guessed that the nursery period in their lives was over and it was their time to move into the main river. I still wonder if the chub and dace had moved into the river after they had been caught by us and other anglers too many times, or even predated upon by the herons that were nesting in a nearby tree or even a land-dwelling predator during the early months of each summer.

It was such a wonderful place to be in the summer, as it was any time of the year. There was so much going on with the wildlife all around me, I often missed bites and only saw my float rising back up to the surface as it floated past from up stream. Much of the distraction was caused by dragonflies as they whizzed and whirled around my head, making me take evasive action and duck away with cautious awareness. I couldn't make my mind up whether the prehistoric-looking things were graceful and beautiful or downright nasty menacing beasts that could deliver a sting of such magnitude that should I be stung, it would kill me within seconds. I was more frightened of these things than any other terrestrial creature, even the soldier beetles, or 'bloodsuckers' as we knew them, that were feeding on the hogweed florets were quite endearing compared to dragonflies.

Grass snakes were another regular visitor to the river bank. They would often swim across the river and slither up the bank as I sat quietly in amongst the thistles and yellow flag irises. Seemingly they ignored my presence as they searched the margins for food before disappearing into the field behind me. Sometimes I got a little concerned when I saw a large one coming straight towards me, thinking it could be an adder, although I knew very well that it would be extremely rare to see an adder swim across a river. It's at these moments when as a kid, you realise you are so vulnerable to the horrors of nature, and the mind begins to work overtime in a scary way. Like imagining being bitten and eaten alive by a viper or being trampled to death by a stampeding herd of cattle, or even falling in, drowning and being swept out to sea where nobody will find you. But then you come to your senses and begin to think about the nice things of nature.

Often I would hear a rustling in the grass and then suddenly a little snout and a pair of black eyes would appear by the side of me, belonging to an inquisitive shrew, field mouse or water vole. A short twitch of its nose and a sniff of my scent and it would quickly reverse away and disappear. I learned that if I kept quite still and didn't even move my head, the little furry rodents would stay a few seconds longer before realising I was there. They were so cute that I quickly brushed off the fear of the horrid creatures that buzzed around me.

Many more trips to Shopham Bridge were made during my school holidays with and without my schoolmates. It became my favourite stretch of the river, with its variety of fishing swims. Being able to fish both banks as opposed to the single bank fishing of Coultershaw, it gave me a different perspective of the river. The dace, chub and perch were in abundance at Shopham but grayling were distinctly absent. I don't ever remember catching a single grayling on this stretch.

Immediately below the bridge was a much wider pool where a more aggressive cast was needed to get to the other side. When you're a young angler faced with an open expanse of water in front of you, you invariably have the irresistible urge to cast to the other side, or at least as far as you can. For some bizarre reason you assume that this is where the fish will be lurking. Even after casting without catching for a while, the temptation to go round to the side you were just casting to and cast to the bank you were just casting from seemed to be the most natural thing to do. And after casting for a while from that bank without catching, you would walk back around and repeat the process all over again. Common sense and discipline have always been an important attribute in angling, but it is only with time these skills are learnt, as I eventually found out.

As the water flowed downstream from under the bridge, the stanchions created back eddies with areas of calmer water. It was here that I finally found fish. Large perch, chub and small barbel would readily take a worm trotted down the edge of the nearside stanchion, in towards the swirl and held in the back eddies. Under one of the arches of the bridge was a ledge where it was possible to walk through, under the bridge and out the other side. This was a great place to shelter from the rain on those wilder weather days, and whilst doing so on one occasion, I spotted an eel swimming alongside the wall on its journey upstream from below the bridge. There was plenty more fishing available below the bridge but I didn't bother going there; I didn't have to, I had plenty of river to go at upstream and I was satisfied with that.

Contented that I was learning to conquer my local river, in my mind anyway, there was another type of waterway I was beginning to learn about, and that was the canals.

CHAPTER 4

The Canals

Throughout my teens, the family would enjoy a barging holiday for a week or two each year on a variety of different canals among the country's vast system. Over those years, I enjoyed 13 weeks of cruising around the Regents Canal, Oxford Canal, Kennet & Avon and the Grand Union Canal. The most important part of my holiday luggage was my fishing tackle – nothing else would matter and I would make sure as much as possible could be packed safely into the car. Fishing was the part of the holiday I looked forward to the most and I fished whenever we stopped, whether it be for lunch or at night time or even just waiting to move up through a lock system. I would get my fishing gear out and have a go, even if it was just for a few minutes.

When we were on the move, I spent most of the cruising

time up at the front of the narrowboat watching the wildlife and leaning over the side peering into the water. The forward motion of the narrowboat sucked the water from the banks, exposing the root systems of the vegetation. In times of lower water levels, especially during periods of drought, the water would completely drain off from the sloping sides, drawing fish down with it. I would see fish of all species being dragged into the main channel of the canal by the suction of the water. Shoals of skimmer bream and roach and even the odd pike could be clearly seen.

These observations gave me a fascinating insight as to where I would most likely catch fish from their preferred natural habitat. The very idea of being able to see them excited me beyond belief. The man-made habitat of this particular aquarium was all very realistic and educational, but for the first time ever I was now seeing the natural home of fish for real. I was beginning to understand that fish did not necessarily keep to the deepest areas but were quite at home in depths of 12 inches and sometimes less.

I continued learning about canals through reading books and visiting the museums on the canal routes throughout the country, discovering that they were all constructed by man and were not at all natural waterways. The structure was very different from that of the river with the uniform depth and would be very still, with a current or flow only occurring when locks were being used by boat traffic. It was a totally different style of fishing, which I found to be a combination of fishing the farm pond and the river. At times my float stayed in a fixed position and at other times it would rush past as it did in the river. I was beginning to learn how to think like a fish and think about how they would react to the changing conditions. I was also thinking about the bait I had thrown in and how it must move with the flow, and so I should fish slightly further down when the flow started and only loose feed during the still moments. It was all starting to make sense, and when I fished the river again I could put these new-found skills to good use.

I was always the first to awake in the mornings and would creep around the boat trying not to disturb the others, although ironically the more I tried to be quiet the noisier I actually was. I would drop things on the steel deck and scrape gear along the fibreglass roof – it was an impossible task, but I tried my best. The dawn chorus was always the best part of the day, when nature began to wake with the ducks and their ducklings appearing through the fine mist rising from the water. The sun appearing over the distant horizon was always a treat to watch, but the best bit was that I didn't have to walk anywhere to witness the serenity of this tranquil rural life, it was literally on the doorstep.

It wasn't always like that of course, it did rain sometimes – many times in fact – but it didn't matter at all, things just got wet and I had to put up with it. The only problem was that when the maggots got wet in their tub, they began to crawl out and when you're concentrating on fishing, you don't notice these things until it's far too late. Oooops!

Over the years the family's confidence with hiring the canal narrowboats grew, and we had many successful holidays without accidents or inflicting serious damage to other boats or crew members. Eventually larger 8-10 berth narrowboats would be hired so friends or other family members could join us on these fun packed trips afloat. Two of the friends we invited the family had known for some years, Maureen and her boyfriend Peter, who turned out to be none other than the fisherman I had first met all those years before fishing for minnows in the Shimmings Brook. He was still very much into fishing and I couldn't have wished for a better fishing companion to have on the canal for a week. We would reminisce about the days on the brook and agreed that it was good fun and how we both had moved on with our fishing, having many tales to tell each other of past failures and achievements.

Now we were fishing together, he fished at one end of the narrowboat and I the other, sometimes catching alternately, sometimes together and sometimes never. Predictably, when the bites were not materialising, frivolity would inevitably break out as it often did when I was with a fishing buddy. I'm not sure if it was just me, but practical joking seemed to follow me around and when anglers had catapults and maggots to hand, many maggots would often go astray in the direction of your companion. But in this instance it didn't last long, as the other crew members weren't as comfortable about having maggots wriggling around the deck and complaints were soon lodged as they awoke to find them in their sleeping bags.

However much fun these holidays were, the angling experiences and newly-gained knowledge of the canals were invaluable to my future angling career. The scaling down of tackle to get more bites was a huge learning curve – even now it is probably the single most important reason why bites are not as forthcoming as they should be.

During those canal years my angling companion introduced me to his brother, Derek, who coincidentally was also keen on fishing. The three of us arranged a day trip to a carp water belonging to Midhurst Angling Club. Never having specifically fished for carp before, this would be my first experience of it. I had never even known Rotherfield Pond existed, even though it was directly opposite my old school, just across the river and encircled by trees. It was summer time and the water was warm with carp cruising around just below the surface. There were quite a few of them exposing their backs out of the water, slurping food items off the top. They looked absolutely huge. Some of them I was told weighed more than twenty pounds. The only time I had seen such large fish was years ago, in a tank at the aquarium in Brighton, but even they didn't appear this big.

There would be no use using fine tackle here and I geared up with 10lb breaking strain line tied to a size 8 hook. Freelined floating crust would be the bait, bought fresh that morning from the local baker's.

By this time my mode of transport was a Suzuki 100 motor bike, gratefully received as a 17th birthday present. It made it so much easier to get to my fishing venues; it was still a bit tricky loading up the basket and rod holdall, but I managed. The others had cars and I couldn't wait to be able to drive, so I began driving lessons as soon as possible. The thought of having a car was one heck of an exciting prospect.

In those days I didn't have the luxury of a choice of rod and reel to change from light to heavy fishing, so I bought a new Abu Garcia Cardinal fixed spool reel specially to take this heavier line, although I would have to make do with the one rod. After passing the hook through the bread and securing it with a twist of line, it was dunked in to the water to gain a little weight and then gently lobbed out into the pond to lie in wait for a carp to suck it down. It was heart-stopping stuff when a fish did rise and gulp at the bread. The floating line would zip across the surface towards the hook on the strike, more often than not terminating with a failed hook up and leaving me cursing and frustrated but laughing along with the others. Mind you, I did give as good as I got when it happened to them.

I couldn't work out if I was striking too soon or too late, but when I did get a hook up, it was exhilarating, as the fish bolted across the pond leaving me hanging on until it tired. I never did catch a twenty, although I had one or two over 10lb, but that didn't matter.

Having thoroughly enjoyed my day as a day ticket guest of my friends, I allowed my Petworth AC membership to lapse and joined Midhurst AC. The three of us had several more trips to Rotherfield and to other waters belonging to the club, having some great laughs along the way. We also had some trips further afield, like a week camping at a Devizes campsite called Lakeside. Funnily enough not much time was spent fishing during that week, only a few hours on the lake and a day on the Kennet & Avon Canal. Even though both sessions were quite successful with us catching skimmer bream and roach, we were all over 18 and the Wadworth's 6X began to take its toll. Early nights to bed and early morning starts went by the wayside after only a couple of days following the discovery of this local brew, and much of the time was spent nursing hangovers and feeling too dog-rough to get out of the cosy sleeping bags and go fishing.

There was, however, one exception. One morning during a horrific thunderstorm, a leaking tent resulted in everything getting a soaking. The camp site was half flooded and some unlucky camper's equipment floated away in the breeze towards the lake – the only thing preventing their belongings from sailing off into the lake were the reeds at the edge.

We were a little luckier in that our tent was pitched on a slight ridge to the side of the camp site, so we suffered only from the torrential rainfall. Even so, this went beyond the peak of our camping tolerances and although much laughter and frivolity was had by all, we agreed that camping was not for us, and it was never repeated.

Someone (I think it was Peter) then came up with the crazy idea of getting a group of lads together to spend a week on a canal narrowboat. After much organisation and unrestrained excitement, the day finally arrived when eight highly testosterone-charged lads, armed with several crates of beer, bags full of goodies, overflowing boxes of groceries and a little bit of fishing tackle, were bundled onto an eight-berth narrowboat.

After the inaugural safety checks and the instruction talk from the boat company, our heterogeneous crew were shortly cruising off into the wild waters of the Oxford canal. There were only three of us who were remotely interested in the fishing side of the holiday. The others couldn't care less, but just engrossed themselves into the party spirit. It soon became obvious to us outnumbered piscators that no serious fishing was ever going to take place during this particular week, so it was a case of, if you can't beat them, join them. It was the same during a second one-week canal barging holiday, when a boat of us eight lads and another boat carrying six girls and my mum and dad jointly cruised the Regents Canal in London.

As the days of our canal holiday went by, the only decent

chance of wetting a line was while waiting for breakfast to be made by a nominated crew member. One morning Peter, Derek and I were casting a line when Alex popped his head out of a window and asked if he could have a go. Sure he could, I said, and I gave him my rod. A few moments later a National Rivers Authority bailiff came along and asked to see our licences. I took the rod off Alex and claimed to be the one fishing, as I had a licence. In fact all three of us anglers had licences, but they were invalid for that area, so the bailiff proceeded to hand out notices for Peter, Derek and myself to purchase one when we got back home.

Feeling dejected and removed from the assembly, Alex put his arm up and shouted to the bailiff "can I have one please?" Surprised at his impromptu outburst, we all fell about laughing as the bailiff duly issued his fourth notice of the morning to Alex. The bailiff walked off grinning to himself, almost certainly more than satisfied with his successful early morning's work.

The fishing never really took off because of all the distractions on board, so my plan to acquire additional canal fishing knowledge was going to have to be put on hold for a while. But I have to admit those holidays did broaden my horizons of the natural world – in more ways than one.

As life moved on with new jobs and new circles of friends, I lost touch with my fellow crewmates and to this day I haven't seen or heard from several of them.

CHAPTER 5

A New Era

The Suzuki bike only lasted 18 months, and six months of that were spent in the garage being fixed due to careless accidents of varying degrees and service negligence; I was never mechanically minded. For an early 19th birthday present, after passing my driving test in March 1977, I was bought a car, a Triumph Herald 1300cc. It was my pride and joy, as now I could drive to my job in Chichester and then Guildford, but more satisfyingly, I could drive to my fishing venues with my gear tucked away safely in the boot. I remained a member of Midhurst AC for a couple of years and returned to the venues, sometimes with Peter and Derek, before taking a break to pursue other interests.

I was a young man with an uncontrollable desire for beautiful young women, and my goodness me, there were many at my places of work, the Army & Navy Department

Stores in Chichester and Guildford. My attentions were focused on a whole new circle of friends. Who wants to go fishing when testosterone levels are running that high and you're out clubbing till all hours of the morning? Five years of not having a care in the world regarding settling down brought me to another change of direction which led me to tour Britain as a roadshow presenter (DJ). That relegated fishing to a very poor second, and I only went a handful of times to uphold my interest in the sport.

I rekindled my passion with angling when I became a member of Portsmouth & District Angling Society in the 1993-94 season following a home move to Southsea. P&DAS was a member of the Hants & Sussex Angling Alliance, an amalgamation of smaller angling clubs including Petworth, Bognor Regis, Petersfield and of course Portsmouth, and it boasted a huge portfolio of waters with a variety of ponds, lakes and rivers.

I was fortunate enough to have a reasonable amount of free time to explore the Alliance's fisheries when my work contracts were located around those areas. I did not necessarily fish these venues to begin with, but I met and chatted to other club members who did. The AGM was the place to meet the people in charge, along with some of the best anglers in the club. Chatting with these guys opened my eyes to other methods of fishing, and I was eventually persuaded to join the match group, whose members not only competed amongst themselves but with other clubs from Hampshire, Sussex, Surrey and Berkshire. I knew that my ability was a long way off from the standard required for competitive fishing, having no illusions that I was anything more than a novice compared to these guys, but I was prepared to learn.

I soon got to know most of the group members, and they happily shared information on the best methods and tactics for fishing the Alliance waters. It didn't take too long for me to realise that my fishing gear was somewhat outdated and to get the best out of match fishing I would need a whole host of new and up-to-date rods, reels, a seat box and most importantly, a pole. Soon I purchased a new Daiwa Harrier 13ft match float rod and a Daiwa Connoisseur medium/heavy 13ft feeder rod, pairing them up with appropriate Shimano fixed spool reels.

Pole fishing was a completely new style of angling to me; previously I had avoided the method because I thought it required little skill in that all you did was place the bait in front of the fish's nose, strike at the sign of a bite, wait for the fish to tire itself and then pull it in. I couldn't have been more wrong, as I was soon to find out. I was told that if I ever wanted to partake in matches, I would need to maximise my catch rate by using faster, more accurate bait presentation techniques if I was ever to stand a chance of winning.

I had to part with some serious cash to buy my first pole, which was a Leeda Match Carp at 12.3 metres long. I also needed a new seat box to enable me to use the pole comfortably, so I purchased a Daiwa Boss Box with an adjustable foot platform. Before I parted with my money I wanted to make sure I was comfortable with the new gear, so there I was on the pavement outside the shop, beside a main road, sitting on the seat box and trying out this pole. The shop owner showed me how to add sections while shipping it out across my leading left knee and adding section by section. I was trying my hardest not to smack the tip section on the ground and break it before it was even paid for. Drivers and pedestrians were giving me some rather peculiar looks as I blissfully waved this 40ft carbon fibre wand in the air.

Somehow I managed to ship out and unship the entire length without breaking any sections and was satisfied this was the way forward. Several ready-made rigs and a whole host of other pole fishing paraphernalia were purchased that day. The shop owner showed me how to elasticate the top two sections with a No.6 elastic and said I would have to elasticate the spare top sections with a No.10 at home.

The nearest pole fishing venue was Hilsea Moats, Eastern and Western, which although in close proximity to each other were totally different waters. They were situated 100 yards from a narrow band of sea water commonly known as the Creek, which connected Portsmouth Harbour to Farlington Marshes. The freshwater moats contained a higher level of salinity than other freshwater fisheries, but the carp were tolerant of this. There was a good head of carp to 20lb in Western and a few large rudd, along with the odd tench. 100lb nets of carp were occasionally caught by regular anglers who knew the fishery well.

The turbidity level in the Western Moat was always far higher than in Eastern, mainly because of the number of carp stirring up the bottom as they fed. As a result of this high turbidity very little weed grew here, with the exception of a few beds of potamogeton, flag iris and bulrush, making it an ideal carp fishery. Eastern however, was very different, in that the water was comparatively clear and contained a large amount of Canadian pondweed, which required management throughout the summer months. The fish stock was very different also, with large tench being the dominant species for the anglers. Large shoals of small rudd were a target for speed fishing practice when the tench weren't playing.

This venue, like many others, was not without its problems. One hot summer the oxygen levels plummeted with a blue-green algal bloom and the fish were struggling to breathe. The Environment Agency was called upon to lend the club some aerators powered by petrol generators. It was a 24-hour operation lasting for several days, and members were called upon to man the equipment day and night until the weather changed.

Naturally I volunteered to do a session. It was a Friday night and I was sitting all alone in my van at the side of the track on the grass verge between the Eastern and Western Moats, guarding the three aerators, which were worth several hundred pounds, against theft or vandalism from the inevitable high-spirited late night revellers returning home from a drunken night out in Portsmouth. As darkness fell across the Hilsea Lines, an 18th and 19th century line of fortification (although earlier defences were built during the civil war of the 1600s), I was thinking I could have been a Cavalier, a Roundhead or maybe just a total numbskull.

The latter was probably the most appropriate in the circumstances. As the first group of swaggering teenagers approached I adopted a friendly and jovial philosophy, thinking this would see me through the forthcoming encounter without undue aggravation. My strategy worked, as the group passed me by with only a few comic remarks on my geographical location, accompanied with some bemused looks on their tired faces as they bid me goodnight.

After that amusing experience the rest of the night passed by peacefully, with only the muffled sounds of nature, the quiet humming of the generators and the distant passing of vehicles on the M27 violating the quietness of night. The hours were long and drawn out, with only the topping up of petrol for the generators keeping me occupied for ten minutes every few hours.

As daylight broke through the trees, the unmistakable aroma of bacon butties and fresh coffee wafting towards me alerted me to the approaching day shift guys. Unfortunately my shift was not over. Disturbingly, the guys had seen many dead fish on the surface of the Western Moat. The aerators were clearly not enough to oxygenate such a volume of water with the high stock levels of fish. It was a sad sight for everyone, but the removal of the carcases was now our priority. There were dozens of dead fish, ranging from 2lb to 15lb. The only way to get to them was for someone to wade in and net them out. For sure that was not going to be me. Fortunately one of the guys had waders, so voluntary selection was not required and the laborious task began.

The decision was made to dump the carcases into the creek for the crabs to devour as they eventually dispersed with the incoming tide. The question was, how could we get the carcases to the creek? Simultaneously four pairs of eyes looked towards my van. I realised that I had no option but to agree, and one by one the carcases were tossed into the back of my empty van. The heat from the morning sun was increasing with each passing hour, turning my van into a mobile oven. The dead fish were fast becoming putrid and could be smelled yards away. I began to wonder if this was such a good idea.

By lunchtime all the floating dead fish we could see were in the back of my van, and with all doors open I drove towards the creek, while the other guys followed on foot holding their noses and gesticulating towards the stinking fluid trailing from the back. I reversed the van up to the creek and the fish were swept into the water, leaving a disgusting blanket of slime and effluvium behind. It took several days for the smell to disperse from the van, and even after many bleachings and washing out with hot water the smell seemed to follow me around for weeks afterwards.

Everything about the operation seemed to be a good idea at the time, but what we didn't take into consideration was the incoming tide.

A couple of days later the club secretary began receiving phone calls from concerned local residents, questioning him about dead carp that were being washed up on the beaches of Tipner Lake and asking if the club knew anything about it. I believe all knowledge of this phenomenon was unequivocally denied. At a future club meeting the volunteers involved were asked to seek alternative methods of disposing dead fish in the future.

Eastern Moat didn't suffer any fish loss at this time because of the difference in habitat with the tree cover protecting the water from the heat of the sun, and algal bloom was not so much of an issue. The fishing here continued to be excellent throughout the summer months with evening matches being a popular attraction. I was now in the early stages of being seriously interested in match fishing at the time, but wanted to learn more about the competitive side of angling.

The only way of finding out about match fishing was to attend a club match and watch from the bank, asking questions from the beginning throughout. I turned up at one of the evening matches and received an invitation to sit with one of the match team to learn about his approach to the water. I probably learned more about pole fishing tactics during those four hours than from all the books, magazines and videos I'd seen and read over the past few months.

It was a fascinating insight to see the different rigs used in different situations for different species. My angling was done with much the same set up for all types of float fishing, other than using different line strengths and hook sizes. The most enlightening message from all this information was that fishing for larger fish doesn't necessarily require the use of heavy lines and big hooks. A double-figure carp could easily be landed on 5lb breaking strain line or less, with a size 18 hook. This was to change my attitude towards rig setups for ever. Another key point was that line diameter is as important as breaking strain, and with the new high-tech pre-stretched lines available it is possible to scale down without compromising strength.

Practice, practice, practice on using the pole was the advice given to me that evening. My mentor assured me that once I had mastered pole craft I wouldn't want to use anything else. I believed him. Every opportunity I had to go fishing, I would take my friend's advice and use the pole.

The very first time out I found it much more difficult on the bank in front of water than on the pavement in the street. With trees and bushes behind me, I struggled to keep it balanced as I shipped it out metre by metre. The total weight of the pole at 12.3 metres was only 910 grams. Not heavy by any means, but as it was the first time I had used a pole, it was an entirely new experience. More often than not the rig would wind itself around the pole tip while I bounced it up and down and shook it side to side, until I realised that if I allowed the float to ride on the water it would prevent the tangles.

The next task was learning how to loose-feed maggots with a pole cup. A small egg cup-sized pot was attached to the tip of the pole and a few maggots tipped into it. The idea was to get the maggots out as far as possible, dumping them into a predetermined area without spilling any on the way. It wasn't long before there were maggots everywhere, in my wellie boots, down the front of my shirt, in my pockets and all over the bait table and rod bag. I just hoped nobody was watching this hideous spectacle. I was laughing uncontrollably to myself as I relentlessly persevered, and eventually I managed a successful bait drop without spilling any maggots on the way out. It certainly was a case of trial and error until I finally mastered the steady rhythm needed to perform the task satisfactorily. When all the maggots finally splashed down on the target area in a tight group it was one of those 'eureka' moments, and I punched the air with triumphant celebration.

I had great fun practising my pole skills with the little rudd, and my highest catch rate was 134 fish in 60 minutes. It was easy to catch half a dozen fish using the same maggot, so a rhythm could be maintained in casting, catching, swinging in to hand, unhooking and dropping the fish into the keep net and then casting again. It was great fun and I learned that several of the matchmen would compete against each other during friendly sessions.

I spent the remainder of the first year of my membership of P&DAS practising and learning about the many waters on the club's books. It was a time of exploration with a whole new tactic that became the pivotal and incontestable approach to my angling. Stillwater or river, the pole was always the 'go-to' method, and I abandoned my rods to their cloth bags, scarcely allowing them to see the light of day for many months.

My skills in handling the pole improved immensely during those months and fishing at the full length of 12.3 metres became second nature in all but the most extreme weather conditions.

The time had now arrived for me to seriously consider entering the competitive world of match fishing, and I booked onto a club match at Sinah Warren Lake. It was a bright summer's day with about 20 anglers preparing for the draw. Sinah was predominantly a carp water and I had never fished it before. I had no discernible idea of how to fish the water or what gear to use.

It came as a welcome relief to me to find out I wasn't alone in this predicament. There were a couple of other first-time match anglers in the group who were, like me, new to all this caper. Although it was a competition scenario, it didn't feel that way. Everybody was mucking about and pulling each other's legs about who had caught what and who hadn't caught what during the previous match. Nothing about the peg draw seemed to be taken seriously, and only the odd one or two anglers cared that much. I later learned that they were the leaders in the match group league table and were competing for top spot. Good pegs and bad pegs were of no importance to me as I hadn't a clue what to do even if I drew a flier.

I remember it being a very hot, bright, sunny day with every angler struggling to get bites. It was not to be a dream start to match angling for me, or any of the other rookies. I caught one little perch of about two ounces and a couple of tiny skimmer bream, while the others faired similarly and the winning weight was only 4lb. Despite not catching a net full, it was a great day out with the group and the camaraderie was honourable with an invitation from the match secretary to join them for the remaining matches of the season.

Becoming a member of the match group was the beginning of a whole new chapter in my angling career. Not every match was arranged on club or Alliance waters; many throughout the season were booked on waters belonging to other clubs from Berkshire, Sussex and Surrey. Having lived in the region all my life I thought I knew almost every water, but fishing these matches would take me to sections of my local rivers I had never given a second thought to. Down country lanes, over gates and fences and across fields I would trek, lugging my tackle in all weather, alongside the other members of the group.

Now I was part of the match brigade and beginning to understand about the blagging rights of winning and the humiliation of losing. It seemed to me that everyone was pumped up with the expectation of drawing a good peg before the draw, only to be instantly demoralised when a duff peg number was revealed from the draw bag and everyone else laughed or jeered. It was all part of the banter though, as the new challenge would be to make the most out of what you were given and to work hard at catching a few fish for self-satisfaction and to score a few league points. The prize money was never a serious motivation for winning these matches, as the winner would only receive about twenty quid for their efforts. It was the points gained at the end of the season which were more important. The top twelve anglers at the end of the season would automatically be selected to fish the nationals the following year, if they were able to.

The nationals were a series of matches entered by clubs from all over the country and broken down into four divisions organised by the National Federation of Anglers. P&DAS were in Division 4. I qualified for team selection in the first year when the upcoming national match was going to be held on the River Nene near Kettering, Northamptonshire. A few of us drove up from Portsmouth on the Friday before to stay overnight in a local hotel. We met up with several anglers from other competing clubs, and the evening turned into quite a raucous occasion. The irksome thoughts of an early morning rise were (literally) diluted by several pints of the local brew, as the evening advanced well into the early hours, until someone remembered the main reason for our presence. The 6 am breakfast time arrived far too quickly for most of us, as we were suffering from lack of sleep combined with a tad too much fizz, but a few mugs of coffee and a full English breakfast soon perked us up before the short drive to the event headquarters.

It was more like a county show had hit town than an angling

match. Tackle stands and food bars lined the approach to the main marquees, where there were hundreds of anglers milling around in eager hopes of a good draw. There were dozens of double-decker and single-decker buses and coaches lined up to transport the anglers to their sections.

Driving my way through the car parking zone, I eventually found the rest of my team mates, who had driven up early that morning. As we talked team tactics and apportioned out the bait, they appeared to be more tired than we night revellers did.

I wasn't sure if it was excitement or nervous apprehension pumping the adrenalin through my body while I waited for my section and peg number. The team captain headed off for the draw and the rest of us carried out final gear checks before loading it all on to our relevant section buses, once we all knew our destinations. The rod holdalls were thrown through the emergency exit on to the floor of the rear seat and piled high, while the seat boxes and carry bags were put in to the luggage hold. It was all organised extremely well with two stewards per bus overseeing the carnage, and on arrival at my section other stewards were waiting to give directions towards our allotted peg numbers. It was a far cry from any other match I had ever attended with the club, and I was in awe of the organisational detail and fluency of the whole event.

The match itself went OK, with a few roach in the net for me, scoring average points, and the team faired much the same as we finished pretty much in the middle of the results table. But the result wasn't the be all and end all of the match as far as I was concerned, it was the taking part in the event that we all agreed was the main objective, and for me the experience was a great leap forward in the world of match fishing.

The successive years with P&DAS brought some of the most memorable match fishing of my life. Entering my second national on the River Trent at Newark and partaking in many local team and individual competitions, I won many along the way and inevitably failed to win a whole lot more.

CHAPTER 6

Relocation

Life can throw many unexpected events at you, along the way and one of the most unforeseen changes for me was relocating to Stockport, Cheshire in December 1997. I went up to do some fishing on the Bridgewater Canal in Manchester, as part of a reconnaissance trip at the end of August for a forthcoming P&DAS national match, and met the love of my life, Beverley, now my long-suffering wife. A fishing widow? No, but I did warn her that if she loved me, she must love my fishing. She did and she still does, bless her.

I renewed my membership with P&DAS for the 1997/98 season so I could fish some of the matches while I was back in the south with work. I had more successes during that year than any other with the club. The evening series held on Hilsea Eastern Moat was my highest achievement of the year. It was a four-match series with a maximum of ten points awarded per match and after three matches I was eleven points clear of second place and didn't have to fish the fourth match as nobody could catch me. I did fish, of course. It was a poor match for some obscure reason with most of the field blanking, including myself, but I went away with the winner's envelope firmly grasped in my strawberry-flavoured, pink-stained hands, because my winning method was sweet-smelling strawberry luncheon meat fished over hemp seed.

The other match series was the Angling Times Avon Valley Winter League, which I thoroughly enjoyed because it took me to parts of the River Wey and the Basingstoke and Kennet & Avon Canals that I hadn't fished before. It was another rewarding series for me, but unfortunately I was beaten into second spot by a mere two points and failed to become top club angler in the league.

I reluctantly left the club the following year to join a more local organisation in Stockport. Stockport & District Anglers Federation (S&DAF) was an amalgamation of many small clubs from the area and was my obvious starting point. This was the largest club in the Stockport area with many more waters to explore. I also found out about a small club that had not long been established by regulars of the local Queen Victoria pub. It wasn't long before I was introduced to the Secretary and became a member of this club as well. It was like starting all over again, as I found myself in no man's land and had to begin the process of learning about the local fisheries around Cheshire. There seemed to be more commercial fisheries in this area than there were in Sussex and Hampshire put together, so I had a lot of choice. I made the decision to concentrate on the fisheries where the pub club fished their matches rather than the S&DAF waters. To be honest I wasn't over impressed with their waters; I thought they were very poorly maintained compared to those I was used to down south.

I spent several months fishing the rivers, canals and still waters in the region before joining in with the organised matches which this little club was conceived around. They rented a short stretch of the River Goyt from a local property owner near the town centre, and I found this interesting fishing. The access point was interesting as well, not to mention hazardous. A gate in a wall opened out over a steep set of uneven steps with no hand rail leading down to a narrow, angler-trodden riverside path. It required two or three trips to safely transport my gear to the six makeshift angling pegs. There was a discharge pipe coming through the wall from an adjacent building that stank to high heaven most of the time. The peg nearest to this constant trickle of effluent, fondly called the "smelly peg" by the members, was ironically the best peg on the stretch, and everyone wanted first choice to fish from it. There was a small shoal of bream and some large perch that lived under a tree stump that protruded out over the river. Everyone tolerated the smell just to catch a few fish, although in the height of summer it did get a bit unbearable when fishing a lengthy session.

It was handy to have a little stretch of fishable water so close to home and I spent several evenings down there, fishing every peg to find out what lurked under the overhanging trees and bushes before entering any "flyer" matches that were held there. Not only did this little club organise local matches, they organised matches and days out much further afield.

The first match I attended with this group was near Newark. The venue was called Cromwell Lakes, and carp and tench were the predominant target species. I drew a corner peg and settled down to fish the same way as I did down south. Meat, hemp or corn on the pole down the edge was my tactic for the day and it proved to be a winning combination. I lost several fish during the day but finished with a weight of just under 28lb. It wasn't a huge weight by any standards, but I later learned it was the all-time club record and as a newcomer to the group, I wasn't very popular with some of the members, having won the first match I had entered. But popularity was never my goal – I just wanted to fish to the best of my ability on the day. Win or lose, it didn't really matter, but being in a competition everyone has to try and do their best, otherwise what's the point in taking part?

My time spent exploring the local waters paid off, with several competition wins under my belt, and at one time it seemed as though I was winning most of the matches I entered, to the dislike of many other anglers. An element of jealousy overshadowed my success, with accusations of cheating around the group. Of course there was no cheating, it was just the fact that on the day I caught more fish and in turn won the matches with a heavier weight. Unfortunately some couldn't understand that, and animosity set in amongst a few of the members.

After a couple of years, in spite of the bitterness that developed among a minority of the members, I became Match Secretary of the group. Unsurprisingly, some members decided to move on to other clubs, but overall the membership increased steadily. Not everyone wished to take part in the organised matches, they just wanted to come along and pleasure-fish the venues I had booked, which was welcomed by everyone. It was more of a day out with the lads for these guys, which had been the original ethos of the club at its inception. But there were a few that enjoyed the competitive side of angling, so I established a league, with a trophy being awarded to the winner at the end of the season. The club didn't have a trophy collection to speak of, only a small shield that would be awarded to the winner of the annual fur and feather match that was held every December.

It was a starting point, but in order to retain interest within the group I decided to expand the trophy collection by obtaining small sponsorship from local businesses. I invited the business owners to donate a trophy to the club which would be competed for during individual matches throughout the season, and my requests were met with great enthusiasm from everyone I approached. A new trophy cabinet was constructed by the pub landlord to house the new silverware and shields. All the newly-acquired trophies would be formerly presented to the winners during a presentation evening at the end of the season.

Money began trickling into the bank account with profits gained from the organised matches, along with football scratch cards which were taken around the pub every Friday evening. Social occasions were well attended throughout the next couple of years and most of the members enjoyed the companionship of like-minded people, so much so that a proposal was put forward for the club to become a member of the NFA in order to partake in the national competitions. There was great excitement and enthusiasm as preparations were drawn up to include a team of anglers in the Division 4 competition on the Nene at Newark. Everything went smoothly and a great weekend was had by all. We didn't finish very high up in the results table, about 10th from the bottom, but nobody cared too much and talk of the following year's competition was high on the agenda.

Regrettably though, not everyone was so passionate about increasing the fortunes of the club, and once again a few became to show animosity towards me, conjuring up an unpleasant atmosphere which overshadowed meetings, so I decided to resign my position and hand the task to someone else. I could only put it down to jealousy because the veterans didn't like it when I became the star of the show, so to speak which seems a common development in competitive angling when the newcomer wins too often. I think the tipping point was the National, when it was decided to have a pooled pot of money for the highest weight returned by a member of the team. I declined, joking that I didn't want to take their money. Sure enough, when the weights were revealed I had the highest of our team members and even though I didn't partake in the pools, there was still an ill feeling amongst a few that I had beaten them again.

During the season of 2000/2001 I approached the National Federation of Anglers with an interest in becoming a licensed angling coach. There was a huge amount of written course work to undertake, with day seminars to attend within the Level 1 and Level 2 qualifications. I had the time and was sure I had the knowhow and experience to become an angling coach, so I signed up.

My introductory session necessitated a visit to Mallory Park Fishery in Leicestershire for a coaching trial, just to see if I could make the grade. The session only lasted an hour and a half, divided in to two parts consisting of an angling skills display and a one-to-one Q & A session, which I passed with flying colours apparently. The next step was a couple of tutorial lessons at Warrington Anglers HQ, where I would enact a roleplay in a coach-to-student scenario and fill in a few session plan forms; that was my Level 1 completed. It was a bit of a doddle really. Level 2 took a little longer as it was more in depth, including several coaching appraisal sessions across the region followed up by an assessment in a real coaching environment at Hampton Springs, Cheshire. A few weeks later I was awarded my Level 2 Certificate in Coaching Angling, all paid for by the NFA. The only financial encumbrance to me were my own personal travel expenses etc.

The Victoria pub-based club collapsed the following year and all the trophies disappeared, while I understand the bank account funds were distributed amongst the remaining members and sadly the club was no more. I thought it a great shame because the club was generally a very sociable outfit, but I think apathy played a huge part in its demise and the old school wanted to go back to the former pleasure days out, neglecting the competitive aspect.

Shortly after leaving the Victoria club I was approached by a committee member of S&DAF, asking if I would consider becoming the Junior Coordinator of the organisation, due to my coaching qualifications. In the first instance I was asked to attend a meeting to discuss candidate expectations of the vacant position. I can only describe the meeting as like attending a job interview for a top position in Her Majesty's Government. I was called in to sit in front of a select committee of top-brass officials to answer a barrage of questions. I didn't know any of the people, and I found it quite amusing during those awkward silent periods when they didn't know what to ask me next.

After much deliberation I accepted the offer in the 2001/02 season and my first job was to write to all the affiliated member clubs with active junior sections informing them of my new position. The federation was run by a typical outfit of a few long-serving committee members who to my mind seemed as though they thought they owned the club and were very reluctant to allow newcomers into the fold. The Chairman and Secretary who had been appointed the season before me were the only ones motivated with a pro-active attitude and keen to see the introduction of new blood on to the committee. During my first committee meeting I felt there was too much dithering and a lot of talk without saying anything, and if a certain person didn't get his own way, he would shout and stamp his feet and threaten to resign. It was so funny. I later learned that this particular gentleman threatens to resign at least twice every year, but as yet he never has done.

Rising above all the petty politics of individuals, my second task was to persuade the committee to re-join the National Junior Angling Association (NJAA) after several years of absence. The reluctance to pay the affiliation fee was evident with the said few, but my proposal was narrowly passed by the committee, so now I could get stuck into the process of forming a junior section.

Travelling hither and thither during my search for junior candidates to partake in the NJAA regional matches, I was met with enthusiasm from member clubs and it wasn't long before we had a team of 12 budding young anglers whose parents were also wishing to be involved. We had some terrific days with the youngsters, taking part in the regional matches organised by the NJAA. The climax was the National, which was held on the Calder and Hebble canal at Wakefield. I hired an 18-seater minibus and one of the dads had a long wheelbase van into which we bundled all the gear, and off we drove to the match HQ. Everyone was very excited, and the laughing and singing on the journey was heart-warming. Nobody knew what to expect of the day ahead, which made it far more of an adventure trip for us all.

On arrival at HQ, the organisation was very much like the NFA seniors' nationals that I had fished with P&DAS, even down to the section transport laid on for the young participants. None of the adults were allowed to give coaching to the young anglers during the four-hour match, so all we had to do was to make sure they all got settled into their correct sections and peg numbers and that was us done until the "all out" was called later that afternoon. It was a very frustrating few hours for us adults as we all wanted to help and give advice, even to those of another team, but we couldn't through fear of getting the lads disqualified. By lunchtime there was only one option available to us, or at least only one we could think of, which was to go to the local pub, where we had a rather nice roast dinner.

At the end of the match I drove to the furthest sections to help those lads pack up and take them back to the HQ myself. It probably wasn't the best idea, because the journey took me down some very narrow farm tracks and over a canal bridge with a sharp bend to negotiate on the exit of the bridge. It was quite easy on the outbound manoeuvre and I managed the minibus exceptionally well and was even congratulated on my driving skills, but the return trip was a different story. Negotiating the tight bend before crossing the bridge required an approach from a different angle and regrettably, I have to say, I got it wrong.

So there we were tightly wedged between the two brick walls of the bridge. A fraught debate ensued on how to get out of this predicament. It was a Catch 22 scenario. Reversing would have ripped the front bumper away from its housing and caused untold hidden damage, while going forward would scratch the van all the way down the nearside to the offside front bumper, which by now was already scratched anyway. The final conclusion we all came to was for me to carry on and hope for the best and accept the consequences.

By this time I had drawn quite a crowd of spectators, and as I slowly eased the bus forward over the bridge the ever-increasing crowd began to cheer like over exuberant football supporters at a cup final. The bridge wall ripped down the near side of the vehicle, removing all the paintwork and leaving long scars of fresh shiny steel in its wake, and the offside front bumper was now hanging off. I was thanking my lucky stars I had paid the insurance excess damage waiver when I hired the vehicle.

It was very embarrassing driving through the HQ grounds with all but a few people looking on and eagerly pointing to the newly-scarred exterior of our minibus. Everyone wanted to know the story, and a few of my passengers were only too pleased to tell all.

The match results seemed to become secondary at that moment, but eventually they were revealed; our lads finished just below mid table. Everyone agreed that the results were encouraging and congratulated the team on their efforts, but the most important thing was that everyone, including the adults, enjoyed a brilliant day out and was looking forward to future association events.

It was another exciting time for me as I got to know members of several local clubs who invited me to present awards to their junior members in recognition of their achievements in club events across the Stockport area. I was also invited to provide coaching sessions to a few that were interested, but unfortunately, successful though they were, the enthusiasm was short-lived with the parents having to accompany the youngsters. Once again, apathy was the underlying obstacle.

New House Farm pool was owned by S&DAF, but the site was an utter disgrace and to my mind an embarrassment. It was totally neglected, with a makeshift den erected in one corner by the local scallywags, and was used for all manner of illicit behaviour. The fishing platforms and pathways were in various stages of dilapidation and collapse, and a serious accident was waiting to happen to some unfortunate angling member, or more probably a local resident feeding the ducks.

It had been this way for many years, and nobody on the committee seemed bothered about doing anything about it. I decided to put a maintenance action plan together, along with the assistance of the bailiff to clear the site, dig out and restructure all the angling platforms and destroy most of the Canadian pondweed which covered 90% of the pool. A small budget of £500 was allocated by the committee towards the project for the reconstruction of the existing platforms, with the introduction of a couple of new ones. Within days of starting work, the entire site looked so different and people began to show renewed interest in to an oasis of nature within a heavily-populated housing estate.

However not all the local residents agreed, as I found out one morning. Across a couple of fence panels that had recently been erected were the words "MIKE FOX IS A W****R" in red spray paint. A touching contribution, I thought, if only they had used my favourite colour of blue!

The work was going well, with 16 angling platform bases completed. All that was needed were for the tops to be finished off with ribbed concrete. For some reason, the idea of using ribbed concrete didn't go along with the ideology of the committee – they wanted me to use square concrete paving slabs, thinking they would be safer. Discussions and explanations about the sizes of the bases not being measured to take slabs didn't seem to hit home, not to mention the unsightly aesthetics. Given the amount of work we had undertaken without any other input from the committee, this needless intervention struck a sour chord with the bailiff and myself. We couldn't understand why they should refuse our proposals of a more permanent and clearly safer finish to the platforms. But the committee's clique of old-timers were not going to budge, and the work never got completed, not during my tenure, anyway. There seemed to be an underlying intolerance to new blood coming onto the committee and getting on with work that should have been done years ago, and if work wasn't done their way, there was no way. It wasn't just with me apparently. I learned that it had been happening for years. Officers of the Federation came and went like football club managers. Whilst I was on the committee the Chairman, Secretary and Minutes Secretary all resigned during a period of 12 months because of the stale and antediluvian hierarchy.

I was now also at the end of my tether and I reluctantly made the decision to resign, leaving the old blood to get on with it. It wasn't just the committee members that were disillusioned with the remaining management committee; individual members and affiliated club numbers were dwindling fast, all them being annoyed, unhappy or bored with a situation that had existed for such a long time.

Then the Vice Chairman of S&DAF and Fisheries Officer of GOSJAC AC asked me if I was interested in becoming the Secretary of GOSJAC because their current secretary had resigned. I thought about it over a couple of months while attending a few meetings before accepting the invitation in the 2004/05 season. I did wonder at times if I was jumping out of the frying pan into the fire, as this club was one of the few remaining affiliated member clubs of S&DAF.

I took on the job more as a challenge than anything else, knowing that they too were pretty stagnant in their ways and finding the administrative side of the club somewhat archaic, with only a handwritten book for recording the minutes of meetings, which were written as an essay rather than an itemised log of discussion. They didn't even have a constitution to abide to. I realised there was an awful lot of work to be done to bring this club into the modern world and to be recognised as a bona fide club with the local authority and national organisations. I was absolutely staggered by the amount of apathy I encountered during my 10 years as Secretary. The club seemed to be run for the few and not for the many of the 107 members, most of whom complained about this, that and the other but did nothing about it. Everyone remembered the good times of the seventies and eighties, telling me many stories of their triumphant days of the past, but now it seemed as though it was all doom and gloom.

My coarse fishing suffered a setback during the GOSJAC years as I became less interested in match fishing, with the commercial carp fisheries being the dominant venue that everyone wanted to fish. It was fun for a while, but the novelty of catching one carp after another after another became, dare I say it, boring. Once you got to know a venue, there was little skill in catching a netload of carp that were huddled together in a huge shoal right in front of you.

The following is from an account I wrote in my blog from 2015.

I was invited to fish a couple of memorial matches over an Easter weekend at Mere Moor near Alsager in Cheshire. This is a commercial venue that is mainly stocked with carp and a place where big weights can be caught in the height of summer. Pole or feeder fishing was going to be the method for me and I was going to stick with one method for each of the days, depending on which pool I drew. Good Friday I drew Pool 1, Peg 1. Dead handy, as I had just happened to park the van right behind this peg before the draw. But even more of a coincidence, I had had a sneaky practice on this peg the day before, so I knew where the fish were, and lo and behold they were still there on this match day. This peg also happened to be rated as the flier on the pool, so I was heckled and jeered by many of the other anglers to the tune of 'Foxy's going to win it, the jammy git' (or words to that effect that I can't publish).

The "all in" sounded and within five minutes I was into my first carp. A fish of around 4lb was safely and unceremoniously dumped into the keep net. Up went the jeers again from surrounding anglers, but I wasn't bothered. I wasn't bothered for two reasons – I knew it was only in fun, and I wasn't bothered about winning. I didn't care if that was the only fish I caught all day. Honestly!

I was there for the occasion and to enjoy a bit of banter and some pole fishing, which I hadn't done for almost a year. All my gear was old and not up to serious match angling pressure any longer, not to mention that I personally wasn't up to it either – six hours sitting on a box is no longer for me.

After the first hour I had five or six fish in the net and I found it was already becoming boring and monotonous. I went on getting fish after fish, but I became less interested in landing them and I let them get away by dropping my pole in the water and letting the line go slack so they got off. Other anglers were struggling, and I could see their frustration as it was clear the fish had shoaled up in my swim under the tree that overhung the left-hand corner where I had found them the day before. After a couple of hours I decided to go for a coffee break and get something to eat, so I had a 30-minute interlude, just to ease the numbness of sitting on a box for all that time.

After that I went back and soon put a couple more fish in the net – not large ones, about 3-4lb each. I soon got bored again and decided to have a walk about and a chat to other anglers, and by now a few fish were being caught from all over the pool. The guy to my right was reaping the rewards of my absence and taking a good number of fish from open water. I returned to my peg after a couple of hours and fished the last hour out, netting one more but losing two or three. I couldn't wait for the "all out", so I started packing up early and was all cleared away by the time the final whistle sounded.

At the weigh in I think it was 37lb for me. I actually thought it would be more, but clearly some of the fish weren't as heavy as I first thought. The guy to my right won with about 41lb and another chap weighed in between the two, so I came third and won £20. It covered my peg fees of £15 and I only used a small bag of micros and a handful of three-year-old hooker pellets I found in my bag which I hadn't used, because when I did try them out I never caught on them.

The Saturday match was on Pool 2. I drew a peg with open water in front of me and to my left and right, so the feeder was going to be the method. I mashed up a tin of out-of-date luncheon meat with a bit of hempseed I had found in the freezer the day before, and that was all I was going to use. I was informed that meat didn't normally catch many fish on that water at that time of year, as I found out for myself after two hours without a bite. That was enough for me to decide on packing up and drying out the gear in the warm sunshine after the previous day's soaking. So that's what I did for the next couple of hours, and everything was put away bone dry.

As this was a five-hour match I hung about for the "all out" and watched a guy pulling out carp one after another from under a bridge to the island. He ended up with 91lb and not surprisingly won the match.

Whilst I enjoyed the two days out, despite the weather being foul on the Friday, this kind of intense match fishing is no longer for me. I do find catching these carp monotonous and unrewarding, and I think it is time to put match fishing behind me. But I can understand that many anglers enjoy it, and why shouldn't they? I did too, until a few years ago.

I thought this poem was brilliant and it reminds me of my match fishing days. It was written by Linda Billington.

I'm Sitting Here on My Box

I'm sitting here on my box wishing things had gone a lot better,

The rain's still falling, all my maggots escaped, and I'm getting wetter and wetter

I hate this peg, I never do well, oh why couldn't I just draw the flier?

This peg's too deep with banks too steep, over there I'd have also been drier.

On pole I've been fishing a small pinkie's tail, on a dinky size 22 hook

A 0.8 bottom to a 0.10 line with a rig that I saw in a book.

The shot are strung out, with a few lower down just sitting above my hook-link

With bait touching bottom, it's a sensitive rig, it's bound to catch fish, so you'd think...

The nets of the guy on the peg to my right look like they're ready to bust

They're bulging with fish, with one more on the way, I look back to my float with disgust

But my float just won't budge, it defies to dip down, not many a nudge have I seen,

But the guy on my left has been pulling them out with a speed that's almost obscene.

He's playing a whopper, it's nearing the net as I sit pulling out handfuls of hair

It's easy a double, the elastic's full out, as I watch near bald with despair

Oh just let it fall off, or let him fall in, either option will sit well with me

'll cast out the method to see if I'll catch, just as soon as I free hook from tree.

Then the bloke on the bank just across from my swim is ready to chuck out the bomb

He flings it with gusto, doesn't feather his cast, it's just like a scene from the Somme!

The fish have all scattered, that puts paid to my plan, I'll just have to stick with the pole

I ship in again and top up the swim, change my rig for big fish now my goal.

My bargains with God have not been heard and it's now nearly twenty to three

We finish at four and weigh in to score, it looks like a bad day for me

Then just as it looks like I've abandoned all hope, my float now drops out of sight

My elastic shoots out, there's a fish on at last, and I ship out my pole to the right.

Just Me and the Fish

*It's going for cover, I'll have to be quick as I add all the sections
to fit*

*And now it's just down to my luck, if it's in, and a matter of
brawn over wit*

*Oh please don't come off, nor hook-point fail, as I dip the pole tip
underwater*

*I hold on in earnest, I hope my line holds and my knots are as
good as they oughta*

*I see swirls on the surface way out on the lake and I start to sweat
and to pray*

*It's now raining harder but that doesn't matter, it's just
getting brighter, my day!*

*Please let me land it, I whisper within me, heart pounding
louder and faster*

*I'm not sure I'll land it, the battle's a thriller, but the elastic soon
shows it whose master.*

*I'm back in contention, bait up and ship out, it's gone quiet to left
and to right*

*But don't think of them now, my float's gone again and I hold
on with all of my might.*

*A stream of fish have come into my swim and on landing are
now in my net*

*I wish I'd changed earlier my tactics and bait, I look back on
my day with regret*

*It's five minutes till all out and it's now gone quiet, so time for a
sip of my tea*

*I look back, in seconds my float's sunk from sight, now my luck
on the day's down to me*

*The all out is shouted, "Fish on!" I cry and a fight for the match
is alive*

*It surfaces briefly, I get the net out but it's away again fast on
the dive.*

It goes into the reeds just down to my left, I'm really not sure that I'll win,

It turns to the lake and I scoop with the net, it's taken and held safe there within

The moment of truth, the scales are brought round and I've now 71 in the net

The guy to my right has weighed 63, and the left hasn't weighed in quite yet

So we walk to his peg and settle the dial and tip the fish onto the scales

The fish start to flap and to wriggle about, spraying droplets from dorsals and tails

I was ready to quit with two hours to go, sitting depressed and feeling quite glum

Freezing my bits, being spattered with mud and sitting with quite a numb bum.

But just as I look back on my earlier spell and what should I , could I have done

They say he's been pipped and weighed 69, can't believe it! They say I've just won!

So if you're a matchman, we've all had those days when the fish just won't take their grub

It's supposed to be fun, but if you're having a mare, remember – there's always the pub!

Linda Billington – A Docklow Dangler

CHAPTER 7

Angling and the Environment

I didn't choose angling – I think it chose me. That sounds a little spurious, but I believe my interest developed not from going fishing but from the fascination of the rural outdoors, especially running water. Water was always an attraction to me when I was young, even little things like soap bubbles in the washing-up bowl and the vortex created by the sink plughole when poured away down the drain. Daft as it sounds, the kaleidoscope of gyrating colours in washing-up bubbles fascinated me.

The movement and motion of nature's watercourses captivated my imagination from a very early age, whether it was from the sea, lakes, rivers or streams. The water cycle of our planet grabbed my attention in the later years of primary school, especially the variety of organisms that thrive in it. Although I didn't study the subject specifically until my grammar school days, biology was always my strongest subject throughout my schooling years, and I particularly showed an interest in aquatic vertebrates and invertebrates. In the clear running water of streams and rivers, the most attention-grabbing signs of life to me were the fish. They might all look like peas in a pod from above, but each fish has its own unique identification characteristics and markings that go unnoticed by everyone except the angler.

I was never interested in catching and killing; for me it is the pleasure of catching, admiring and then releasing a wild creature that otherwise would go unnoticed. There is of course so much else to see when out fishing. The godfather of angling, Izaac Walton, wrote in his book *The Compleat Angler* that we should "study to be quiet". Total quietness is something many never get to experience in today's bustling world of high drama. Constantly rushing around to fit everything into a short working day with deadlines and financial targets that have to be met in order to appease the boss. Modern life creates noise everywhere which we all take for granted and accept in our daily lives. Being quiet is difficult for some people and noise is inherent. They seem to be quite incapable of settling into quietness unless they are fast asleep, and even then they are probably talking in their sleep – or snoring!

There are very few places in this world nowadays where quietness is absolute. The closest we can get to it is away from the madness of civilisation and out in the countryside. If you study to be quiet, nature will come to you and you will see things most people won't. The bright blue flash of a passing kingfisher or the leap of a brown trout as it devours an ascending mayfly in mid-air. When out fishing you will also hear things that many people will ignore. Invariably you will hear a buzzard before you see it soaring high in the sky. Tree boughs creak as the wind blows through woods and the breeze rustles through the bankside vegetation at your side.

You will feel things that many people never will. Close your eyes for a few seconds and feel the line from your reel tighten and the rod tip bend as you cast. Imagine the heart-stopping moment when you hook into a fish, feeling every lunge and shake of its head in its bid for freedom.

You will smell things that many people never will. Wild garlic and water mint growing on the bank evoke memories of home cooking. Fields of rapeseed waft their sweet scent of honey and mustard through the air. The not-so-sweet aroma of the farmyard typifies rural life at its best and always awakens the senses.

Then there are the expectations, the disappointments, the successes, the failures, the laughter, the camaraderie, the solitude, the companionship, the glorious warmth of the summer sun, the bitter cold of the winter frosts. The rain, the wind, the sleet and snow all add to a pleasurable fishing trip, which is sometimes an expedition but always an experience, making every day different from the others, if sometimes exhausting.

I often wonder if those folk who misunderstand angling, imagining it to be a sedentary sport, are those that have never given it a go. Golf isn't for me, but I have given it a go on several occasions before finally arriving at the conclusion that I wasn't any good at it. I could flippantly say that golf is nothing more than swatting a little ball as far as you can, chasing after it and poking it down a little hole in the ground. But I understand that there is a whole lot more to it than that. I scored 147 on a 9-hole course once, shame I wasn't playing snooker really, but I had such a laugh doing it. I'm sure more people would enjoy angling if they would allow themselves to.

The streamlined hydrodynamics of fish to an angler could I suppose be compared to the aerodynamics of an aircraft to an aeronautics engineer, a thing of beauty, and they are beautiful. So many iridescent colours creating spots, stripes and flanks of light reflecting mother of pearl. How can anyone not marvel at the wonders of fish that have been designed by the evolution of nature over 450 million years? They should be revered for their ability to thrive under adverse conditions throughout their lives. From the egg stage to mature adults, the fish run a gauntlet of obstacles and obstructions in order to survive not only nature's unforgiving elements of predation, parasites and diseases but the intervention of humans.

Pollution, which comes in many forms, is a sore point with me. We think of pollution being all about chemicals or effluent spilled into watercourses from our manufacturing industry in urban areas, but it also derives from farmland waste and the fertilisers and insecticides that are sprayed onto our food crops. Pollution is also caused by thoughtless individuals who litter the countryside by dropping cigarette butts, cans, plastic wrappers and containers, bottles and sweet wrappers etc. They may be small items by themselves, but collectively they are pollutants and a serious threat to fish, wildfowl and to all other creatures that inhabit our waterways.

Fortunately there are organisations (too many to mention) which work tirelessly to protect and restore waterways for the enjoyment of generations to come. If only our generation would stop and think a little more before discarding waste out of the car window or leaving food wrappings behind when out for a stroll.

Regrettably, we do have anglers amongst us who are just as guilty of leaving litter, which includes discarded fishing line with weights and hooks still attached. I find it all the time on the bank, whether it's a commercial fishery or a stretch of rural river miles from anywhere. I like to think anglers' litter is more accidental than deliberate, but a little more thought from everyone would go a long way in protecting our fisheries.

References taken from the Environment Agency remind us that pollution is not only from large scale sources. Domestic households are just as guilty. Sewage is another name for waste water from domestic and industrial processes. Despite strict regulatory control, the Environment Agency data shows that the water and sewage industry accounts for almost a quarter of the serious water incidents in England and Wales over a period of 12 months. The agriculture industry covers 76% of the land area of England and Wales. Agricultural processes such as uncontrolled spreading of slurries and manure, disposal of sheep dip, tillage, ploughing of the land, use of pesticides and fertilisers can cause water pollution. Accidental spills from milk dairies can also affect the quality of water.

Every year there are about 3,000 pollution incidents involving oil and fuels in England and Wales. Oil spillages affect water quality in a number of ways. Oil can make drinking water unsafe to drink. A substantial amount of oil released into oceans and seas will destroy wildlife and the ecosystems that sustain them. Oil spills also reduce oxygen supplies within the water environment. Radioactive waste is another source of water pollution. Radioactive substances are used in nuclear power plants, industrial, medical and other scientific processes. They can be found in watches, luminous clocks, television sets and x-ray machinery. There are also naturally-occurring radioisotopes from organisms within the environment. If not properly disposed of, radioactive waste can result in serious water pollution incidents.

Lots of people dump supermarket trolleys, bicycles, garden cuttings and electronic waste into rivers or river banks. This is illegal and offenders may be charged for fly-tipping if caught. River dumping not only causes water pollution, it also harms wildlife and increases the risk of flooding.

Happily it is not all doom and gloom. If we work together and think twice about discarding our unwanted wares, who knows – we might even save our planet yet.

Over the years my angling life has taken me off in several directions of interest. I have discovered that angling is not all about catching fish. It is also about caring for the environment and protecting it from destruction, either by the uncontrolled growth of vegetation or wanton ruination by us humans in the desire to make more money.

I was invited to attend a series of workshops organised

by the Environment Agency at Reaseheath College, Cheshire. The workshops would cover the topics of Invasive Species, Parasites, Pathogens, Fishery Law Enforcement, Habitat Reconstruction and Protection and General Fishery Management duties. The invitations were sent out to all regional angling club secretaries, and being the secretary of GOSJAC, I thought it would be an ideal opportunity to learn more about fisheries, especially as GOSJAC had an almost derelict fishery at Heaton Mersey which needed restoration. The reservoir at that time was called Mellands. It was on a piece of land that belonged to the local industrial estate landowner and leased to the club on a free to use "goodwill" agreement with no official leasing contract between the two parties.

The fishery at that time leaked like a sieve and from recordings made in the club minutes, the committee had been discussing what to do about it for 13 years. Nobody had come up with a solution in all that time, except for patch rendering a retaining wall with waterproofed cement and topping the water up from an adjacent borehole with a pump that looked as old as Stevenson's Rocket. If the situation wasn't treated as hilarious it would have been embarrassing. I wanted a stop to all this malarkey and proposed a rehabilitation plan for the reservoir. My idea was met with a wall of negativity and apathy from the committee and members and I was told that the club was not big enough and we couldn't raise the funds needed to undertake such a task. I have to admit to scoffing at them somewhat, letting them know that I could do it, but it would take time and the club would need to make some kind of financial undertaking. They had the money to make a contribution, so why not?

They finally agreed to let me have control and get on with

sorting the problem. There were still a number of people who remained negative, insisting that I couldn't do it, but this only gave me more of an incentive to achieve my ambition.

At the same time the Mersey Basin Campaign (MBC) movement was in the grips of the clean-up of the River Mersey system from its source in Stockport to New Brighton where the river meets the Irish Sea. By pure coincidence, or luck, the MBC was in the early stages of obtaining a huge grant from the European Union to fund the design and construction of the River Mersey Nature Park, utilising land adjacent to the river from Stockport to Heaton Mersey. Sadly GOSJAC's reservoir didn't fall within the boundaries of the proposed park and could not be included within their project.

However, as a representative of an interested group (GOSJAC), I was invited to the many public meetings the MBC was arranging to keep the local community updated with its progress. During one of these meetings, the leader of MBC approached me about the reservoir, having heard about my proposals. She invited me to attend a Greater Manchester Water Forum to be held in Manchester Town Hall and give a 10-minute 'soap box' presentation during the event to raise awareness of my project and gain some professional help and advice.

The day came and I had my pre-written speech tucked away in my pocket. Dozens of people from across Greater Manchester had gathered in the main assembly room of the Town Hall. They were leaders from the regional councils, Greater Manchester Police, the Environment Agency, water companies, recycling firms and several other environmental bodies.

The time came for me to take the podium, having

witnessed others stumble nervously through their speeches. Someone told me that if I imagined my audience to be naked, it would take my mind away from the public-speaking fear factor. Well, it settled my nerves all right – when I was asked the meaning of GOSJAC and where it came from by the forum's chairman, I just began to giggle. It broke the ice and I proceeded with my speech, which went down a storm, and I was rewarded with a huge round of applause at the end. Phew! That wasn't so bad.

After the morning's session I was approached by a qualified environmental management team and an executive from the Environment Agency, who offered to support me with the development of the project, and the rehabilitation of Heaton Mersey Reservoir was born. It was to be the beginning of a great deal of research work for me in the coming months.

The first task was to draw up a feasibility study and assessment of the proposed solutions and design of a new fishery to aid the necessary funding applications.

The following is the environmental assessment carried out by Aquatic Management Services on behalf of GOSJAC AC.

Environmental Assessment and Rehabilitation Report

A detailed environmental survey and examination of Heaton Mersey Reservoir was undertaken in order that recommendations could be put forward for a rehabilitation programme to be advanced. The aim of the study was to provide the level of detail that would enable constructive decisions to be taken on longer term reinstatement of the water and to help secure funding for the programme of work.

For any particular site it is desirable to undertake an environmental assessment in order to guide the planning and management of that water and surrounding land. By so doing, this serves the following purposes.

1). It provides a document that is a reference record for long term actions.

2). It enables objectives and priorities to be determined to enable structural management decisions.

3). It gives a basis for the management resources to be better targeted and also enables specific additional resources to be justified and achieved.

4). It provides a continuance of planning action.

INTRODUCTION TO THE PROGRAMME

- THE PROGRAMME
- HISTORICAL ASPECTS
- IDENTIFYING THE NEEDS FOR THE PROJECT
- PUBLIC CONSULTATION
- ENVIRONMENTAL ASSESSMENT
- ANGLER AND USER REQUIREMENTS
- RESERVOIR IMPROVEMENTS AND FEASABILITY
- THE WORKS

These are the main areas that are to be addressed in the investigation.

1). Consider historical information on the lake design and operation

2). Provide depth profiling of the lake and substrate assessment

3). Assess the general biology of the lake and consider any particular issues or problems.

4). Assess scope for the facility to be developed as a fishery

5). Assess arrangements for water level control

6). Provide guidance on landscaping for the lake and its surrounds

7). Prepare a structured programme for improvement

Mike Fox

HISTORICAL ASPECTS OF THE FORMER BLEACH WORKS

The cotton industry was a major industry in the 19th and early part of the 20th centuries and, as a consequence, many mills were built in Lancashire and Yorkshire, where there was a large population that could supply the workforce for the rapidly expanding industry. Stockport was one such area that benefited from such industrial development and the infrastructure was soon created and brought great prosperity to the area. This involved the construction of the Manchester Ship Canal, the Port of Manchester, the development of the Port of Liverpool with its then ship building industry and also expansion of other industries such as coal mining.

The working practices depended not only upon the manufacture of cotton within the cotton mills in Lancashire and elsewhere, but also printing and dyeing of the cloth before shipment or disposal for retail. The legacy of the industry, however, is that the cotton and dyeing industry was dependent on availability of a plentiful supply of water for the processes involved and this was one of the key reasons why the North of England was so suitable. Although quite wet in the North for the most part, there needed to be reliable water to ensure there was continuity of manufacture. The mill constructed at Heaton Mersey was a cloth and bleach works, which has now long since been demolished with the site redeveloped with light industrial and office accommodation.

By the 1930s, with the fallout of the Second World War and the increasing pressure from cheap imports from abroad, the cotton industries fell into serious and eventually terminal decline. The mills were progressively demolished and with them all the infrastructure fell into disrepair and abandonment as well. Many of the mills and other company businesses have long since disappeared, often replaced with housing, but a good number of the mill lodges have survived, although large numbers have been sadly neglected on account of shortages of funding to reinstate them. Their original use disappeared with the demise of the mills, but a growing requirement for leisure facilities on water space is an important driving force for their re-establishment.

In most cases it is reasonable to suggest that once the lodges have been lost, they will not be resurrected, which would be to the detriment to the local community.

Originally several lodges or reservoirs were present at the time when the Heaton Mersey Mill was fully operational but now only one remains – Heaton Mersey Reservoir.

In recent years there has been a resurgence of interest in re-establishing old, often derelict waters and waterways because the true value in both ecological and environmental terms has been found to be undervalued. A typical example of this is the re-establishment of the canal networks around the country, which have not only recreational value but ecological and amenity value as well. There is an equally justifiable argument for saving the majority of the mill lodges and related water bodies, because not only do they provide an essential recreational facility for the urban communities to use and enjoy, but the ecological and amenity value of these facilities can individually make a significant contribution to enhancing wildlife and habitats in industrial areas.

IDENTIFYING THE NEEDS FOR THE PROJECT

- A health and safety risk
- An unsightly environmental hazard
- Regeneration of a disused and derelict area
- A lack of existing local facilities
- Enable GOSJAC AC to engage with the wider community
- Enable GOSJAC AC to work with local and national agencies
- Encourage good health, wellbeing and education

ANGLER AND USER REQUIREMENTS
PRINCIPLE OBJECTIVES

1) Provide an established, balanced fishery
2) Creation of a unique, fully accessible community facility
3) To enable GOSJAC AC to engage with local groups
4) Promote a wide range of skills among participants

PUBLIC CONSULTATION RESULTS

435 members of the community across all age groups were consulted about the project and have given their full support. Local schools and community groups have been informed and have indicated their intension to use the facility for educational projects.

PROJECT FEASIBILITY AND
IMPROVEMENTS

1) The water is large enough to provide an excellent angling venue. Approximately 25 pegs could be provided around the reservoir.
2) The additional facility in Stockport will provide an opportunity to attract more anglers to fish in this area.
3) At present, the water with its soft, exposed sediment at the margins is a health and safety risk and therefore with re-instatement it becomes considerably safer.
4) The lake can be re-lined to make it watertight.

5) The potential water depth, even with lining and contouring, is excellent for a fishing venue for leisure, teaching and competition events.

6) The grounds surrounding the lake can be enhanced to a level where it will provide a unique ecological and amenity for the local community.

7) With special consideration, but with relative ease, the water can be made totally accessible to a large number of disabled anglers.

DRAINING AND FISH REMOVAL

Before the water level was allowed to drop too low the removal of the remaining fish stock was to be considered. It was thought unlikely that there were many fish present, as low water levels would have made them easy prey for predators and low oxygen levels would have killed them. It was impractical to use conventional netting methods and electro-fishing was the only way. This resulted in a surprising 171lb of carp and 63lb of silver fish being removed.

In respect of the Heaton Mersey Reservoir, a structured

programme of change needs to be adopted but rather different principles apply from many other waters. This is because the facility has specific health and safety issues that need to be addressed along with the measures of re-establishing it as a fishery. At the present time there is low public awareness of its existence, but this could change with careful management and improved landscaping. A further aspect that needs to be borne in mind, however, is that it could provide a useful, additional angling water and, thereby, complement the facilities for the local community.

The reservoir was once one of a number of pools that formed part of a bleach works water storage system. The works has now been demolished and the reservoir is the only pool of the network still remaining. In the more recent past the water has operated as a leisure fishery, but it was found that the upper water retention level was not possible to achieve except by pumping from a borehole. With time even this facility became more difficult to maintain and subsequently the reservoir was allowed to fall to its natural level and angling activities declined. During wet weather and at times of saturated ground conditions, water retention improves, but it is only a temporary situation, because as soon as dry weather prevails, most of the water drains away.

The reservoir is rectangular in shape and is approximately 70m in length and 45m wide and stands in an area of approximately 1.3 acres (0.526ha). The water is now almost fully drained from the reservoir although a few centimetres remain. The depth and the profile of the water are almost constant throughout. There is approximately

30cm of sediment lying on the bottom, although this is deeper in some places. Bank height is approximately 2.5m and therefore, with lining, a water depth of around 2m could be achieved with possibly 2.5m in some locations, although due consideration of a new clay lining would have to be made. Embankment width is approximately 3m around 3 sides and 10m at the north-eastern end, where there is a containment wall.

As has already been mentioned, the depth of water in the reservoir has rapidly decreased due to a suspected leak, in addition to cessation of water being pumped into the reservoir. The drop in water depth will have a number of impacts including extreme variation in temperature and dissolved oxygen levels, making the water unsuitable for sensitive aquatic invertebrates and fish at the present time.

The exposure of sediment from the reservoir bottom is providing an opportunity for aquatic and marginal plants including pioneering celery-leaved buttercup. The invasive Himalayan balsam is also beginning to appear in large numbers around the damp exposed material. As the water is currently only a few inches deep it is likely that the water body will be rapidly lost due to the ingress of vegetation, most probably becoming a reed mace swamp with pockets of yellow flag iris and Himalayan balsam, before succeeding to willow and alder carr woodland. Although this habitat will favour some species, the BAP habitat eutrophic standing water will be lost in a very short space of time.

Blue-green algae has been a problem on this reservoir, most probably due to periodically elevated nutrient levels. The removal of decomposing organic matter and the establishment of a more diverse range of aquatic plants should reduce instances of algal bloom and minimise drastic changes in oxygen levels, as will increasing the overall depth of the reservoir.

When the reservoir is dry there is approximately 30-45cm of sediment/rubble etc to be removed from the whole of the bed, which will constitute between 950 and 1500 cubic metres weighing up to 3500 tonnes. To save on cost of movement of this material off-site, most is to be relocated to a settlement lagoon at the north-eastern end. This area is approximately 45m x 9m with an average depth of approximately 1.5m. This will give a carrying capacity of approximately 600 cubic metres. There is calculated to be a shortfall on storage at the location, but it is intended to raise bank height and width of the bank at the north-eastern end in order to hide the containment wall structure, and to allow free and safe access around the lake. Storage for sediment could also be accommodated at the corners of the lake and in areas of the site where uneven ground exists. In addition, it is possible that a new island will be constructed to allow sanctuary for wildlife that will become attracted to the new water space.

INLET AND OVERFLOW CONSTRUCTION

Before the construction of the inlet and overflow chambers could begin, a survey of the respective locations was to be carried out. We learned that an existing culvert lay possibly somewhere to the north-eastern corner of the lake and served as an outlet to the original working reservoir for the bleach works. This was eventually located in the neighbouring field. It was found to be in sound order and could easily be reinstated as an overflow outlet for the new reservoir to the river Mersey.

The construction of the existing borehole was surveyed and then disassembled to allow for a new borehole pumping system to be installed. A steel container was to serve as a secure housing unit for the pump and generator and for other tools required for the sustainability of the fishery.

As there would be changes to the bankside pathways and fishing pegs around the pool once the water was re-established, it was important that the layout was designed so that less able-bodied anglers from the local community and elsewhere could share the benefits of the fishing venue. We had to give a little forethought to how this could best be achieved, particularly with access around the lake and the fishing pegs that were to be constructed.

DISABLED ANGLER AND USER REQUIREMENTS

Angler Peg Construction. These should be constructed in the same way as the pathways and lead directly off and to the same level without any step. A 200-300mm gap should be allowed to the waters edge to allow for anglers to insert bank sticks. They should be of 1.2m depth and 1.5 m wide and have a raised kick board to the front edge. Surfaces should be level, firm and non-slippy in all weathers and definitely not slope towards the water. They should be of a height no greater than 30-60cm above the water surface in order for anglers to land fish safely.

As there will be changes to the bank side pathways

and fishing pegs around the pool once the water is re-established, it is important that the layout is designed so that less able bodied anglers from the local community and elsewhere could share the benefits of the fishing venue. For this to be achieved a little forethought needs to be undertaken on how this could best be achieved, particularly with access around the lake and the fishing pegs that are constructed.

Access Pathways. The main requirements need to minimise steep or bumpy walkways and access points. In general, footpaths should be a minimum of 1.5m wide. Pronounced cambers to paths should be avoided with central cambers being preferable. Gradients should not exceed 1:12.

Surfaces to pathways should be firm, non-slip and possibly slightly textured. To blend with the surroundings 'Crusher Run' grit stone blinded with a 5>dust topping is to be used. Rough muddy ground and gravel or shingle will be avoided, as they present difficulties for wheelchairs.

APPOINTMENT OF CONTRACTOR

1) Seek suitable and experienced contractors
2) Arrange for quotations in accordance with project requirements
3) Accept quotation and confirm its inclusions
4) Agree phase commencement and completion dates
5) Obtain relevant access permissions from adjacent land owners

So there it was. The proposals for how to proceed with the rehabilitation of Heaton Mersey Reservoir were all in place, except how it was all going to be funded. Was it all an unrealistic hope, a pipe dream, a fantasy, or could it really be achieved? There continued to be doubters and cynics amongst the membership, but most were in favour of proceeding with the idea and for me to lead the way.

I put it to the members that if they wished for a sub-committee to be formed, volunteers would be welcome, so decision making could be shared. Nobody came forward – not even a member of the club's management committee wanted to have any involvement with the indeterminate procedures that were sure to follow. Secretly I was pleased nobody else would be involved with the administration of the project. There would be no need for unnecessary meetings or phone calls, no arguments over decision making and most of all, no delays in the process. I actually believe the majority either didn't think it would happen or didn't have a clue how to go about it. It was all going to be down to me, success or failure. Although I had it firmly fixed in my mind, failure was not an option and never would be. I alone would report back to the club at the monthly meetings, keeping everyone informed of the progress being made step by step.

THE FUNDING PROCESS

Once the estimated figure, plus a contingency, was established from quotes received, the dilemma was – where is the £106k going to come from? It was prudent for the club to make a substantial contribution, considering the amount of funds it had at its disposal. The initial cost of the land purchase and access rights would have to be supported by the club before any consideration of external funding applications could begin. I put the motion to a club meeting of spending the £6,000 to cover the cost of land purchase and legal fees. The mixed response I received was highly amusing, to me anyway. The doubters were all there in their little group at the back of the room, shouting that no way should the club spend any amount of money on a piece of disused, derelict land out of town. Their thoughts were that if external funds were not forthcoming, the club would be stuck with 1.3 acres of waste land of no use to anyone. It was a perfectly reasonable objection on its own merits, but I had a trump card up my sleeve. I had already been in talks with the Environment Agency regarding tapping in to rod licence funds for a grant of £40,000 to be awarded over two years. Although no guarantees could be given, the likelihood of the club receiving this money was very high, given the sustainability of the project. A complete change of attitude was strikingly obvious amongst the members, with nods of approval escalating in to murmurs of positivity throughout the room. Ironically, some of those members disagreed with the idea of paying a rod licence fee so they could go fishing in the first place!

With £40k from the EA and £6k from club funds, there was only another £60k to find. If the club contributed an additional £10k then the serious task of searching for the remaining £50k would be much easier. Eventually, after much persuasion from me, it was agreed in principle that if the £50k could be found, then the club would indeed contribute the additional £10k required.

The aquatic management team which provided the environment assessment suggested they could help in the process of applying for the first stage of funding through a

National Lottery distributor. Relief overcame me after this gratefully received offer, though I hadn't got a clue about the filling out of these application forms with the precise wording preferred by the grant assessors. However, there was a condition expressed that should funding be awarded as a direct result of the applications, Aquatic Management Services would be obligated to carry out the works. It all sounded very fair to me, especially as I had never done anything like this before, and I was totally bewildered by the complexity of questions within the application forms. It was so much easier with the EA – I just wrote a letter to them outlining the project details and how much I needed and they wrote back with their agreement of financial support. It couldn't have been easier.

Within a couple of weeks the application form was completed and forwarded on to the Big Lottery, and the waiting began. The amount requested was £26,500, which would cover the cost of the inaugural stage of the project of clearing and preparing the site. During the waiting period, which was two months, I researched other funding agencies besides the National Lottery. I was keen to accept an invitation from Stockport Metropolitan Borough Council to visit their central offices to privately access their funding finder website. I found myself in the hub of Stockport Metropolitan Borough Council's computer room with full access to hundreds of funding organisations around Great Britain and Europe. Probably the world, if I delved a little deeper into this mind-boggling instrument of cyber information. I was amazed at the amount of money that could be obtained from so many sources should a project fall within the criteria of the funder.

After many hours searching I found a couple of funders that could be worth pursuing, BIFFA Awards and Groundworks UK, which seemed to be the only viable funding solutions to my project needs. There may have been others but I think I would have needed a week to search the amount that were listed on this data site. The facility was there for me to use for the week as the regular user was on holiday, but I thanked the manager for the time I had been allowed, uplifted in the knowledge of seeing for myself the vast number of funding streams available to tap into if I so wished.

Back home, working on my computer, I researched the websites of Biffa and Groundworks, realising that the Heaton Mersey project fell well within the eligibility of both their funding criteria. I wasted no time in starting to fill out the first stages of application forms. Having experienced the first round of applications for the Lottery with the management team, I found these two forms relatively easy to follow and understand. However, there was an element of administrative compliance that GOSJAC at this point would not qualify. It was the lack of documentation regarding policies in terms of environment, health and safety and child protection. I had to quickly draw up and present these documents to the club in order to include them within the funding applications.

Timing was such that these newly drawn-up policies could be presented to the up-coming annual general meeting to be included in the constitution before being presented to the funders.

Soon after the AGM, a letter from the Lottery arrived with

their decision on my initial application for the first phase of works. It wasn't good. They had refused the application on the grounds that it didn't fall within their particular funding criteria for the chosen category and regrettably couldn't fund the project.

Disappointed with the decision, I parted company with the management team and decided to go it alone. It was nothing more than a setback which I shrugged off, and I wasted no time in sending the other applications off to Biffa and Groundworks. The deadlines for these applications were fast approaching and I didn't want to wait for the next round of awards to be offered, as I might lose the funding offers that I had already received from the EA. Timing was all important now.

I couldn't just sit around waiting for those decisions to come back, either accepted or declined. In any event, I had to assume that they were going to be accepted so I could think ahead and be ready to move the project forward with each phase falling into place at the right time of year, both for seasonal benefits and fitting in with the EA financial periods. Good forward planning was essential for the project to run smoothly.

I first heard from Biffa a few weeks later in a letter similar to that received from the Lottery, although it was a little more encouraging. They had arrived at their decision by awarding points across eleven elements of achievement to the sustainability of a green area accessible to the public. Out of a maximum of 33 points the Heaton Mersey project scored 27. The explanation given was that because part of the funds requested was for the construction of the pond before the access pathways were installed, they were unable to fund that particular stage of the project. However, if funding for the pond were to be guaranteed by another funder, they would reconsider the application for the pathways during a future round of awards when the pond itself had been completed.

The sticking point was the EA funds would only pay for part of the pond construction, as it was coming in two instalments spread over two financial years. Obviously the pond had to be constructed before the pathways could be installed, so that scenario was out of the question and the Biffa application was shelved.

The whole future of the immediate start of the project now rested with the Groundworks UK application. A couple of weeks later I received a letter from Groundworks informing me that the application for stage 1 of the application had been accepted and that a representative would be in touch to help proceed to the next stage 2. It was a huge relief to know that a funder of this significance was interested in the project. I had requested £27,500 from this funding stream, which would be combined with the first £20,000 from the EA to fund the construction of the pond.

A meeting was arranged to discuss the logistics of delivering the project on time and within estimated budgets. Imagine my delight when the representative suggested that if Groundworks could fund the full outstanding amount that was required to complete the project in association with the EA, my application was more likely to be accepted in full rather than in part. The maximum the fund would provide was £50,000, so together we arrived at a figure of £49,999 by rearranging some of the phases with the added extras aid sustainability once the project had been completed.

By totalling up all the figures of £40,000 from the EA, the

£49,999 from Groundworks and the £10,000 from club funds, I had enough to commence the project in the autumn of 2008, but only if Groundworks accepted the amount requested. A nail-biting period of suspense passed very slowly until in August 2008 I was extremely relieved to receive the letter of acceptance of the full amount requested. It was only then I knew the project could go ahead as planned and it was all systems go.

29TH NOVEMBER 2008 – PROJECT COMMENCEMENT DAY

Once the waste material was removed from the bottom of the reservoir, a full examination of the integrity of the bed could be made. The bed would then be levelled to a depth determined by the soundness of the substrate, shaped and contoured with the construction of a new island, compacted and then lined with clay. We planned to line with clay the shaped banks around the lake so that the margins would have a safe profile in all areas. Vegetation would be encouraged to develop in the margins and island in order to develop the ecosystem within the water column. After filling, that would encourage the provision of a spawning medium.

The bed of the reservoir would be laid with appropriate clay to a depth of 30cm which would extend over and around the bank edges as well. In essence, when the lining was installed it would be a naturally-contoured water feature and would provide a facility that would provide both recreational and ecological diversity.

LAYING OF THE CLAY LINING

2600 Tonnes (130 wagonloads) of blue/ yellow clay was brought in from farmland in Mobberley, Cheshire. This clay was evenly spread all over the lake bed and embankments to a depth of 30cm and compacted down by heavy roller. Special consideration was given to the aquatic ecosystem, and water-lily beds and fish spawning beds were constructed and levelled at different heights to the outer and island shelves.

Logs were then placed onto the island to encourage insect habitat development within the decaying bark and in turn encourage bird life.

PUDDLING-IN

The puddling-in process began with water pumped in from an existing borehole constructed in 1994 in the north-western corner of the site at a rate of 6,012 litres per hour. An abstraction licence was granted by the Environment Agency to take water from the nearby river Mersey at a rate of 68,400 litres per hour.

NATIVE MARGINAL AND AQUATIC
PLANTING SCHEME

There is no standard list of plants which is appropriate in every pond. Instead planting schemes ideally be both restricted to the plants which are already growing in the locality and appropriate to the physical and chemical conditions.

Planting schemes should always take into consideration the provision of a good habitat for pond animals. This means focusing on species that grow well in water and which therefore provide a good underwater structure for aquatic animals. In addition to the aforementioned, consideration has to be made to the habitat of water fowl, and so plants that are not necessarily recommended due to evasiveness are excellent for shelter and nesting.

The planting scheme has taken into consideration all these factors and comprises of the following.

Marliacae Carnea (Water Lily) Deservedly popular as it is easy to grow and produces a profusion of 8" diameter pale pink, fragrant flowers. Young leaves are purple on top and dusky red below, maturing to green and 8" in diameter.

Nurphar Luteum (Brandy Bottle) Relative of the water Lily, which will tolerate moving water and a

degree of shade. It produces 3" yellow flowers above large 12"x10" green waxy leaves. Some

submerged leaves are almost translucent. Individual plants reach 5ft across.

Filipendula Ulmaria (Meadow Sweet) An indigenous plant growing to about 3ft high and producing feather spires of scented creamy white flowers from June to August.

Myosotis Scorpioides (Water Forget-me-not) Produces mid to dark green oval hairy leaves on sprawling hairy stems that have a reddish tinge. Pale blue flowers with yellow centres are produced throughout the summer. Will grow in full sun and partial shade. Height 6"-12" and will grow in moist or wet soil or water up to 2" deep.

Caltha Pulustris (Marsh Marigold) The native king Cup which flowers in early spring. This daffodil of the pond world and as cheering on miserable late winter days, is happy in wet mud or up to 4" of water over its crown. Prefers full sun and will make a clump of up to 1 ½ ft across and 1ft tall. Harmful if eaten.

Mentha Aquatica (Water Mint) This is a very vigorous pool side plant which when in flower in a large pool situation having spread to form a large clump is quite spectacular. It will grow to 2ft and has a distinctive mint smell and produces a profusion of lilac coloured flowers in ball like clusters. Will grow in moist soil or in water to a depth of 6" and is happy in full sun or part shade.

Lythrum Salicaria (Purple Loosetrife) Makes a tall wild flower that grows naturally on banks of streams and around ponds. It has strong upright stems, topped in summer with long, poker-like heads of bright purple-red flowers.

Iris Pseudacorus (Yellow Flag Iris) A strong large clump forming indigenous plant, producing broad sword shaped green leaves, and in early to mid-summer rich golden flowers followed by a brown seed head which later splits to shed its large pea sized seeds which will germinate quite easily. Height to 5ft when mature and will tolerate up to 1ft of water over its crown.

Typha Latifolia (Great Reed Maice) This plant is often mistakenly called the Bulrush. This is a rampant plant when planted directly into the soil. It is however very architectural and with care can be contained. If left it will spread indefinitely. The leaves are long and elegant. The seed heads are carried on tall strong stems and will stand all winter. It will take up to 3ft of water.

Scirpus Lacustris (The True Bulrush) A native plant producing stiff needle-like leaves that reach to 4ft high. Produces clumps that gradually expand.

Special planting consideration has been given to the island owing to its man made construction. Only shallow rooted shrubs and smaller, slow growing trees would be suitable. The main reason for creating an island feature is to create a waterfowl habitat to provide a safe haven from predators such as foxes, stoats and weasels. Shrubs that produce dense foliage and a crop of autumn/winter berries are favourable, giving the reason for the following choices.

Sorbus Aucuparia (Mountain Ash or Rowan) **Betula Pendula** (Youngs Weeping Birch)

Cornus Sanguinea (Common Dogwood) **Prunus Spinosa** (Blackthorn)

Berberis Lologenesis Rosa Rugosa(Dog Rose)

Berberis Verruculos Mahonia Media (Charity)

For a little colour early on in the year, spring flowering bulbs have been planted around the upper edges of the banks.

English Bluebells

Pinocchio Tulips

Mixed Double Daffodil

LAKE PERIMETR PLANTING SCHEME

The outer areas of the site require a low maintenance planting scheme, but also interesting enough to encourage the non-angling community to walk around and enjoy the flora and fauna that will inhabit the lakeside. Flowering shrubs are largely to be avoided due to the falling of blossom into the water and in the long term have an adverse effect on the water quality and in turn detrimental to angling. Planting annual and bi-annual plants will require excessive maintenance and are also to be avoided. As there are many deciduous trees bordering the area more consideration should be given to grass seeding and spring flowering bulbs.

The following spring flowering bulbs have been planted around the site:

840 Trumpet Daffodils King Alfred, St Kaverne, Goblet, Mount Hood, Bravoure, Pink Charm, Best Seller.

750 Large Flowering Crocus Flower Record, Joan of Arc, Pickwick, Queen of the Blues, Yellow Mammoth.

30 Mixed Double Daffodils

30 Pinocchio Tulips

1600 Single Snowdrops

WATER PUMPING REQUIREMENTS

GEOLOGICAL FEATURES. The site is located at approximately 35m AOD at the bottom of a southerly dipping slope from Heaton Mersey village which is at approximately 67m AOD.

The south of the site is bordered by the River Mersey. The

site is located over First Terrace Alluvial deposits associated with the river which are identified as being sand and gravel deposits. The sand and gravel is water bearing and lies on top of pebble beds of the Bunter, Triassic Period. A solid geological boundary is indicated as passing beneath the pond area indicating that the Manchester Marls underlie the site on the south-eastern side. From the geology it is observed that the sand and gravel is an unconfined aquifer overlying the porous Pebble Beds. Since no aquilude/aquitard is present the water regime of the drift and bedrock is linked and forms a continuous unconfined aquifer down to the Manchester Marls beneath the Pebble beds.

BOREHOLE CONSTRUCTION. It was agreed that a 150mm diameter shell and auger borehole be sunk in the north-western corner to confirm the required strata was present. Following confirmation of the required strata a 300mm borehole was bored at the same position, fully lined through drift deposits to a depth of 21.5 metres below ground level to bedrock. Water was struck at 4.85m below ground level. A test pump was sent down to a depth of 9.00m to draw at a rate of 0.63 litres per second. After 3hrs of pumping the drawdown of the water level was measured at 8.18m at a discharge rate of 5.14 cubic metres per hour.

BOREHOLE PUMP. When the groundwater level is below the surface by more than 6-7 metres, a submersible borehole pump is required. The electro-submersible borehole pumping unit consists of and electric motor which is designed to operate under water, the internals being filled with water for lubrication and cooling purposes. This arrangement prevents any contamination of the pumped liquid. The motor is close coupled to a multi-stage pump which discharges in the rising main at the head and flow required. The chosen pump for this particular project is an EBARA 4" Winner, capable of pumping at a rate of 21 cubic metres per hour at ground level. It has been set at a depth of 15 metres below ground level, which will provide a head discharge of 11 cubic metres per hour.

AERATION SOLUTIONS AT
HEATON MERSEY RESERVOIR

A dual system of 0.5hp Splash agitator aerators have been installed. Each aerator will produce 2000 litres of oxygenated water per minute.

POWER SUPPLY

An enquiry was sent out to United Utilities to provide a quote for a new single–phase electricity supply to the site. Following a survey the quote received was in excess of £10,000. This was found to be too excessive and impractical for the estimated usage and therefore declined. The alternative solution was to be a generator with sufficient output to power both the pump and aerators simultaneously. It should be robust, yet transportable. The chosen generator was a Clarke FG5100ES. Petrol fuelled 13hp engine producing a maximum power output of 5.5 kVa with a fuel tank large enough to run for 12 hours or more.

The finished pool in March 2010

GRAND OPENING

A clause in the funding agreement with Groundworks UK was for the club to hold a Grand Opening Event once the physical works were completed. The date was fixed for 3rd April 2010. An additional fund would be available to cover costs for this day and also organised coaching events in the future to help promote public awareness of the new fishery. Groundworks specified the day was to be publicised as much as possible throughout the local community with posters and fliers, so I had a dozen posters and 1000 fliers printed. I invited Anne Coffey, our local MP to officially open the venue, not for political reasons but because she has shown support in the club with particular interest in the project from the outset. The EA attended with their mobile promotion unit advertising their recent work with flood defence to the river Mersey embankment. A Level 2 angling coach from the Angling Trust accompanied by 3 Level 1 assistants would provide one to one coaching to visitors.

The day was a great publicity success for the club with over 80 visitors attending the event, keeping the coaches busy with several people signing up for new membership.

OBLIGATIONS

Of course no amount of money is ever handed out to organisations willy-nilly without some kind of future sustainability plan. Apart from the satisfactory compliance of the funding criteria, further obligations to manage and maintain the project for years to come is another undertaking for the funding recipient. In agreeing to accept the Groundworks UK funding I was required to sign an undertaking of a 4 year management programme to maintain the fisheries "accessibility to all" promise. Even though the land was now privately owned by the club, the stipulation was that it must be kept open to the public for a minimum of 6 days per week throughout this 4 year period. Accessibility to walkers and wheelchair users was a priority, so all pathways and access gates were to be kept open and clear, grass verges were to be kept to an acceptable height, litter to be picked up and angling platforms to be kept available at all times. To substantiate my visitor number estimate that I stated in the funding application, a quarterly head count of users was required. But without 24hr surveillance, general walkers passing through the venue, would be a difficult, if not impossible task, so an average of witnessed usage was recorded, plus a realistic measured increase during each period. Angler day ticket sales and increased membership numbers were easy to record by income receipts. The evidence of membership numbers were encouraging, with a 60% increase during year 1 and year 2 season and the day ticket sales increased by over 200% during the same period.

Considering the huge amount of apathy and doubt from members in the first instance, The Rehabilitation of Heaton Mersey Reservoir was a great achievement for the club and put them in the forefront of public awareness within the Stockport angling community. For me, it was a great experience and indeed a learning process from beginning to end. In the early stages mistakes were made and obstacles overcome with the application process. But with a little determination, sometimes stubbornness and a lot of confidence, I proved this kind of project can be achieved by anyone if the ambition and willingness is there in the first place.

CHAPTER 8

Angling Tuition

Having a Level 2 accreditation in coaching angling to my name, I wanted to further my experiences in utilising the qualification. It appeared to me that the NFA and the recently-formed Angling Trust were not very proactive in engaging their qualified coaches with a significant amount of angling events, certainly from my perspective anyway. Although I had renewed my coaching licence with them every year from 2001-2012, I was only ever engaged in two events and one of those I organised for S&DAF. I couldn't understand why I didn't receive any kind of communication throughout the years, except those reminding me of the annual renewal of my coaching licence, which naturally incurred a fee. My impression of the Angling Trust coaching scheme was not inspiring me to bother with them any longer, so I decided to go it alone and develop my own coaching platform.

This was more of an experimental idea to find out if there was a demand for angling instruction in the Stockport area. Regrettably, age creeps up on us all and I wondered if some financial gain could be made from my investment with the qualification during retirement. Not that I was ready for retirement quite yet, but my thinking was directed towards speculating to accumulating for my latter years. Searching the internet, I found that several other Level 2 qualified coaches had set up websites advertising their services as angling coaches, but none in or around the Stockport area.

I was keen to develop a website of my own that was clear enough for people to read without the complications of clicking on an untold number of links and sub-headings to find the required information. I located a web developer based in London who specialised in the design of angling-related websites, and with his expertise we constructed a site that was not only aimed towards the beginner of coarse angling, but as an added attraction, those interested in fly fishing for trout. I wasn't qualified in the field of game fishing, so I enlisted the services of a qualified GAIA casting instructor to deliver lessons to candidates who wanted to learn fly-fishing. Ironically, most of the enquiries I received were from people who wanted me to show them how to put a fly out on the water. I had only been fly-fishing for a couple of years, so I explained to them that I was not a qualified fly-fishing instructor. This didn't deter them, as they were just happy to learn the basics. In the event of them wanting to advance, the professional instructor would always be available.

The coarse angling tuition took off at a steady pace with several enquiries from individuals, young and old, signing up for the odd couple of hours here and there on several venues around the area. The series of structured courses we offered didn't seem to be of interest to anyone despite the hugely discounted rates. Candidates only wanted to learn about the practical side of rig set ups and casting accurately to a given spot, rather than learn about watercraft and the whys and wherefores of coarse angling.

In addition to the new website I advertised the angling school by distributing flyers in several nature centres and town information bureaus around Stockport in an attempt to drum up some interest from the wider non-angling community. This exercise worked as far as website hits were concerned, but it had very little impact on tangible enquiries regarding fee-paying tuition. Enquiries from scout groups, youth clubs and junior angling clubs were steadily forthcoming, but they were only interested in my voluntary services under the guise of GOSJAC AC. This was all well and good and generally I didn't mind giving time, it goes with the territory. But in all honesty I formed the School of Freshwater Angling (Stockport) hoping to make a little bit of money, or at the very least, break even.

On several occasions I succumbed to gentle persuasion (partly in the name of self-promotion) to deliver a series of one-hour classroom-style interactive demonstrations to discerning local youngsters who seemed to be enthusiastic about fishing. These developed into voluntary practical lessons on a local club water for a few hours on a Saturday morning. Enthusiastic as the youngsters were, the equipment they brought with them was probably hand-me-downs from their granddads and pretty much useless for the task at hand.

It became obvious to me that if each youngster was going to learn a particular method through my teaching, then I was going to have to supply all the relevant tackle required for that particular task. The youngsters would be dropped off at a venue by their parents and collected at a pre-determined time, two or three hours later. When some of the parents persisted with later and later collection of their children, I soon got the feeling that I was being used as an unpaid child minder. The majority were very good though and some stayed for the sessions, learning a little themselves. I took great pleasure in taking youngsters with learning difficulties and autism. They were great characters and showed so much interest I almost forgot they had difficulties. Their parents were astonished at the level of concentration they showed for what could often be several hours at a time.

It wasn't only youngsters I began coaching, as many adults also wanted to learn about the techniques of the sport. Most had tried a bit of fishing but had had very little luck in catching. It was purely a case of refinement of tackle in relation to the size of fish that were present in their waters. They needed a level of understanding of how to balance the tackle correctly, and that you don't need 5lb breaking strain line to catch a 5lb fish.

On one occasion a gentleman engaged me to teach his grandson the basics of angling, as he had been trying to teach him without success. I took them to Heaton Mersey Reservoir, where they had been themselves several times and had caught nothing. We sat down on a peg where the grandfather openly admitted that he had blanked more than once and was intrigued as to my approach on catching.

After explaining the rudiments of my method, I sat his grandson down by my side and we fished together. Only a few minutes had passed before the fish found the bait and the lad began to catch lots of small carp, tench, perch and roach. He was thrilled, and his granddad was flabbergasted. The two-hour session passed only too quickly for the lad and he wanted to stay a little longer, so I obliged, but after a while they had to go and both granddad and grandson went on their way more than satisfied with their newly-learned skills, especially as I let the lad keep a 4mtr whip along with the rig he was using to catch all those fish that morning. Once again it was merely a case of "Tell me and I will forget, show me and I will remember, involve me and I will understand", the phrase I used to head my website pages.

The fulfilment of catching lots of fish does not always materialise, as a young lady discovered one summer's afternoon. Her partner had ordered a gift voucher for two hours' instruction on a water of her choice, always a difficult challenge for a coach. However, her choice of venue was S&DAF's New House Farm pool in Bramhall near Stockport. I had fished this pool many times before when I had been a member of the organisation, but that was years ago and things can change on a fishery within weeks, let alone years. I knew there were plenty of fish in the pool, but I knew nothing of their exact location and which peg would be best to try. I wanted my client to try all three angling methods of pole, waggler and feeder fishing during the first hour, so she could choose her favourite method and concentrate on it for the second hour.

She arrived on time, as keen as mustard and looking

forward to catching her first fish. The usual practice of telling, showing and then involving continued through the first hour without a single bite, or even seeing any fish movement whatsoever. It was very unusual and quite disconcerting, as something should have happened. I began to question my abilities in the tactics and tackle set-up I had provided, but I was convinced that the lack of interest from the fish was nothing to do with that. The session came to a conclusion after two hours of hard fishing without a fish. I was bitterly disappointed for my student client, but she seemed happy enough with what she had learned and understood that the fish do not bite all the time.

As I was packing away the gear the S&DAF fishery officer arrived and couldn't understand why we hadn't caught, confirming that the current stock levels were good. A couple of days later I discovered that there was a problem with the oxygen levels when the fishery had "turned over" (a term used when a problem with a water develops) and most of the fish had come to the surface gasping for air, while many perished. Emergency aerators were brought in to resuscitate the surviving fish, but it is a sad fact of fishery management that the first visible sign of low oxygen levels is not until the fish struggle to breathe. At least that cruel twist of fate lessened the frustration of my coaching session, which should have produced a fish or two on an otherwise pleasant afternoon.

The most satisfying moment when coaching newcomers to angling is when they tell me they have really enjoyed their lessons and want to spend more time with me. OK, we can say that's good for business, and in some instances, yes it is, but more importantly what I do is not necessarily for profit.

I received an enquiry from the foster parent of a young man who had learning difficulties and attention deficit hyperactivity disorder (ADHD). The request was for me to deliver three one-hour lessons spread over a period of a couple of weeks to find out if the lad would engage with me and angling. Previously he had shown an interest in fishing by watching other people fish and seemed to be calm and relaxed when sitting by their side.

A date was arranged for me to have a meeting with him (his name was Aaron) and his foster parents to discuss his needs and develop a rapport prior to any bankside sessions. Following confirmation of all the necessary administration requirements a session was arranged at Heaton Mersey Reservoir, subject to weather conditions.

The day arrived and fortunately the weather was good enough, although it was a bit cold. Aaron arrived with his foster parents, really excited and looking forward to the session. He had never seen a pole, let alone used one before, so this would be a whole new experience for him.

I thought a length of 8 metres would be ideal for him to begin with, taking into account his physique. He managed this well and found it quite comfortable to use, and after plumbing the depth at several different places he was soon fishing. Bearing in mind we only had one hour, I was keen to get him catching as quickly as possible, so instruction on rig set-up was going to be left for another session. It took only a few minutes before his first bite indication was seen on the float. He struck with a little too much gusto and a small perch came bouncing out of the water, became detached from the barbless hook and swam away. Aaron instantly knew what he had done wrong and told me so. "Next time I won't strike so hard," he said, and we laughed.

Many more bites followed and after successfully landing several small perch and roach he was beaming with delight. He was beginning to ship the pole out and catch fish as though he had done this many times before, so I thought it was time for him to have a go at feeding from a pole pot placed at the tip of the pole. A small pot the size of an egg cup was attached and half-filled with maggots and micro pellets, and following guidance and instruction he shipped it out without spilling any of the contents. I can honestly say that this was the first time any of my students had successfully done this on their very first attempt, so that was a great achievement.

The hour quickly passed, and Aaron was already looking forward to his next lesson, which was to be at his home, where I could show him how to make up a pole rig, a waggler rig and feeder rig. An hour would not really be long enough for him to take in and understand everything, so a compromise on the pole and waggler rig was made. I gave him a 4mtr whip and he made up a canal waggler rig to keep and use on his local canal at his leisure.

The setting up of the rig was straightforward, but it was important that he also understood the practice of plumbing up. Having practised this task in our previous session at HMR, I wanted him to see for himself what was happening below the waterline by the use of a rig tube. These I find excellent for students to get a good idea of shotting a float down and seeing the rig underwater, although tweaking is required when actually using the rig. Following this task I showed Aaron how to make a feeder rig. Aaron's attention to this session was impressive, so I gave him an extra half an hour of my time and he was already looking forward to our next meeting.

Our third and final session was to be on GOSJAC No.2 reservoir at Edgeley, Stockport. This session was to concentrate primarily on using the waggler and feeder. I arrived and set up the rods in readiness for Aaron's arrival and again he was very prompt and had brought along the whip and rig that I had given him at our previous session. I explained to him that the whip wouldn't be suitable for this venue because of the structure of the lake and that the fish tend to be further out away from the banks. He accepted this and understood the differences between HMR and this venue.

Aaron began with the waggler rod and after I had shown him what to do, he took to it and cast extremely well. With extra guidance from me on how to sink the line, he was soon confident enough to strike at bites and re-cast. Unfortunately he didn't connect with the bites and failed to catch on this occasion. Reassuringly, he understood the reasons – having too much slack line and not being quick enough with the strike.

After half an hour it was time to use the feeder rod, and again I showed him what to do and then he took over. His casting ability was good, gaining excellent distance, and like the waggler, in time he achieved regular accuracy. I had hoped for him to catch something during this session, but that wasn't really the day's objective. It was to get Aaron acquainted with using balanced tackle and the skills of using it to his best ability, in which he succeeded.

Whilst Aaron was practising with the feeder I tweaked

his whip rig by adding a couple more no.8 split shot to make the float sit perfectly in the water so it would be ready for him to use on his local canal.

So these three one-hour sessions to introduce Aaron into coarse fishing were very successful, leaving him wanting more. His foster mum said she was amazed at how he had taken to the sport and recognised how he showed so much concentration, learning so much in such a short time and how his personality changed, as he became calm and composed throughout the sessions. Not only were our objectives met, they were exceeded. It was mission accomplished, and it is for that reason alone that I do what I do.

CHAPTER 9

Shameless Self-Promotion

I suppose at some point many anglers would like to attempt a bit of journalism or internet blogging, that now being the most accessible platform these days to share experiences with other like-minded individuals. I'm no exception, but it's finding the time to sit and put pen to paper, or finger to keyboard in this case. It's just an account of my day's activity to save, remember and share, and if anybody takes the time to read them and can relate to my outings, that's great. If not, so be it, who cares.

I hope you enjoy reading a selection of my angling experiences from coarse to game.

Mill Farm

I don't get the opportunities these days to get out and fish anywhere near as much as I would like to, and I know I'm not the only one. Every Christmas time I take a few days out and visit family in West Sussex and Hampshire, and the gear always comes with me in the hope that I get a chance to revisit a venue where I know I will have a decent day's fishing. Mill Farm, near Bury, is such a venue. It's a bit of a risk to suggest you will be guaranteed to catch plenty, but at this venue I have never failed to consistently catch throughout a five-hour session, even in midwinter. I don't think I have ever hit the magic ton in December, but I can honestly say I haven't been far short on several occasions.

With so many well stocked, or perhaps over-stocked, commercial fisheries that are match fished almost every day of the week, it's great for me to visit a venue that is well stocked and not overfished.

The venue is a three-lake complex. Hammer Pool is a match lake where keepnets are allowed. Mill Pool is the

pleasure lake and to the back of this is the Specimen Pool. The complex nestles just to the north of the South Downs in the heart of the Sussex countryside.

After a 10-minute drive from my digs in Petworth, I arrived at 8 am and the air temperature was a fresh 4.5 degrees. Overnight there had been a little light rain but this had cleared, leaving a beautiful clear, sunny, but chilly morning. There was not a breath of wind whatsoever at this time.

As I got out of my van and closed the door, the peaceful tranquillity was shattered by a commotion on Hammer Pool. Three cormorants had been catching their breakfast, but now they hastily disappeared into the sky over the far end of the pool. Maybe they thought I had a 12-bore with me – alas I didn't. Despite the visit of these menacing predators there were many small fish topping, producing spirograph-effect circles on the now calm surface. I knew I would catch plenty of small silvers on this pool, but I wanted a few carp as well and was armed only with my trusty old Daiwa Connoisseur medium/heavy feeder rod. So I chose the Mill Pool pleasure lake.

The swim I chose I hadn't fished before, but I wanted to keep my options open to fishing in open water and also tight to the island. I knew that on this pool the carp tend to stay in open water at this time of year, where it's a little deeper but it's still only around five feet deep. My markers would be the left-hand tree in the picture and to the point of the island. There is a shallower area that stretches from the point to about 75 yards to the left where the owners are attempting to establish a lily pad bed. By a sheer fluke you can see in the photo a line in the ripple on the surface where the shallower bar is.

It is on this line that I was hoping to land my feeder/bomb. I say "hope" because I would not be using my line clip. The reason for this was that the carp ranged from 3lb to 24lb and as I would be using 5lb direct mono as main line and 0.13 hook length to a 16 wide-gape hook, I didn't want a break off if I hit a lump. I know, I know, this sounds a bit heavy for this time of year, especially when using maggot as bait, but believe me you don't need to go any lighter here. Three maggots on the hook will tempt any of the fish in this pool.

My bait selection was maggot, micro pellet and pure brown crumb. Groundbait is banned on this venue, but the bailiff does allow me to use pure brown breadcrumb in the feeder. I like to be simple and not complicate things, either with rigs or bait choices. The rig would be a twizzled loop about 450mm from the feeder where a 450mm hook length would be attached. The feeder would be attached by a swivel link so I could change from cage feeder/maggot feeder or small bomb, and that was it, no fancy leger stops, beads or links where the hook length could tangle around during the 40m chuck.

The crumb would be mixed fairly dry so as to explode during the drop in the water, leaving the maggot and pellet to fall to the deck. Because of the large head of small silvers in the pool, my thinking was that they would come up to the falling crumb and leave the carp to forage around on the bottom. Ha ha ha! Not necessarily so, but it's a good theory anyway.

The session began just after 9 am with a couple of chucks in quick succession to open water. It only took five minutes before I was getting an indication from my tip that fish were about. I had, incidentally, cut my tip back to the second eye and Tippexed the top. I do this because I find that even the heaviest tip can be too soft when wanting to chuck out a large groundbait feeder and it's still sensitive enough for delicate bite detection, so I use it as an all-round tip and I never have to change it. Simple.

It wasn't long before the tip ripped round and I was into my first carp. It made a steady slow run to the right and felt a decent size. The fight was not hectic, but it didn't want to come to the surface until after 4 or 5 minutes it gave up and came to the net.

It was this very lean mirror of about 3-4lb. It was a bit of a sorry-looking fish and not of the usual quality I had caught in the past, but it was a fish and gave me confidence in a good day ahead. At least they were feeding. I put out another cast to the same spot and almost immediately there were small indications on the tip, and then nothing.

I left it for a minute or two and still nothing, so I retrieved it to find the maggots had been sucked out. Little roach or skimmers had clearly found the feed. I didn't mind as it was a pleasure day and any fish will do at this time of year. I wasn't going to scale down just to catch those little fellas and chance losing a carp. Out went the feeder again and a similar reaction occurred on the tip soon after the feeder settled, so I struck straight away and in came a small skimmer. This performance repeated itself several times.

After an hour without any further signs of carp, I decided to cast to the island. The exact same response was recorded on my tip, but I didn't strike, but just left it for a couple of minutes before retrieving again. I could feel a resistance on the rod tip which was not characteristic of just an empty feeder returning. As it came to the surface I noticed a little silver flash following on behind the feeder. Although I was fishing treble maggot on a 16 hook, this little fella had taken the lot and I needed a disgorger to retrieve the hook. It did bring a smile to my face.

Several roach and skimmers followed, but not as small as previous "specimens". These were up to probably 6oz. I changed over to a maggot feeder and cast back out to open water, hoping that the carp had turned up in numbers, and I was rewarded with a couple of mirrors in quick succession, so I stuck with the maggot feeder. Half an hour passed without much action until a terrific pull round on the tip produced this gorgeous looking common, and I couldn't resist taking a picture of it in the winter sunshine. This I thought was a perfect specimen of around 4lb.

Several carp and a few more skimmers and roach followed in an action-packed couple of hours. Lunch time was approaching, so I had a break and wandered off to have a look at the Specimen and Hammer lakes. There was an angler on each, but I couldn't be bothered to walk around and have a chat to see how they were doing, so I just stood and admired the scenery and listened to the wildlife. This was pure heaven, so different from my usual day of fighting my way through the mayhem of everyday life in Stockport and Manchester. I have to say I do enjoy that as well, but it is nice to get away for a while and just enjoy the diversity of nature and appreciate what this country has to offer.

Well, back to the fishing. Same tactics as before, a couple of cage feeders of crumb into open water and a change to maggot feeder brought a few more carp almost instantly. I didn't latch into the doubles that this lake can produce – the largest I had was a 7lb mirror – but at least I had kept myself busy, and that's more important to me than anything.

Time was getting on and my five-hour session was coming to a close. After sitting on a Boss Box for five hours my bum starts to get a bit numb and I get fidgety and want to move about, so I was thinking about calling it a day anyway. Apart from a short visit by the bailiff my only companions for the day were two hungry robins which I had been steadily feeding with maggots, and they seemed quite happy to stick around. I then noticed that the larger of the two had caught a worm and without any hesitation, I'm almost sorry to say, I thought, "Ah perch bait!" So embarrassingly, all by myself, I frightened off the bird and grabbed the worm before it could make its escape. Come on now, we've all done it!

Excitedly and with renewed vigour, I changed the feeder for a bomb and put the worm (the tail end of which had already been bitten off by the robin) onto the hook. The most likely place to pick off a perch would be near or under the willow to the right of the island. I had caught several large perch on the other side of the island during previous visits... I think you know where this is leading, don't you!

The cast would possibly need to be at least 50 metres, so I changed my position on the box and prepared to cast. Because I had changed my casting position I had to contend with the overhanging tree above me, so I kneeled down on the ground and in doing so the bomb and worm sat back down on the ground behind me. The next thing I knew was the robin swooped back out of the tree and tried to nick the worm back off me, so I quickly cast out without any degree of accuracy and thought of distance, and oops – straight into the trees on the island it went. Definitely was time to pack up now.

Eleven carp and about 25 or so roach and skimmers was a reasonable day out for December and I thoroughly enjoyed it. All in all it was a fantastic day.

Heaton Mersey Reservoir

After all the festivities of Christmas, I was itching to get out and catch a few more fish locally following my adventure to the south coast a couple of weeks before. I had a few hours to myself whilst the wife was at work earning some more pennies to keep me in the lifestyle to which I had become accustomed. The weather forecast was not good with heavy rain and gusty winds promised by the Met Office, so it was going to be a trip to Heaton Mersey Reservoir. Surrounded by trees and scrub, the water is quite sheltered from high winds and even with torrential rain, fishing can be quite pleasant for the discerning angler with a good brolly.

A trip to the local tackle shop to buy some fresh maggots and I was off. The van air temp gauge was reading 10 degrees, which for the end of December was quite balmy considering at the beginning of the month it had been -2 and -3, which had left a thin layer of ice on the water for several days.

I arrived at Vale Road shortly before 9.30am to find no sign of civilisation whatsoever. The industrial estate offices and warehouses were still closed for the holiday period, but more unfortunately for me, the burger van was absent. On went the thermals and waterproofs and I backpacked the gear and trudged to the water, thinking I must be mad, but I was full of great expectations of catching one or two of the carp that I had stocked at the beginning of the month. The wind was blowing from west to east, creating quite a lot of turbulence on the surface at the far end of the pond, but it was calm and comparatively sheltered at the near end at pegs 26 to 22. I knew there would be no point in walking too far round so I settled for peg 26, the first one I came to.

This peg produces all year round because of its features. Just to the left is a lily pad pod which protrudes about 8 metres out and slopes off to 5ft deep and this is the point where I would be "laying" my rig, just off the slope at 8.5 metres. I have said "laying" deliberately, as this is totally the wrong thing to do. Many people have complained to me about the amount of weed in the pond and say they don't

get bites and consequently blank quite often. (The weed is *Potamageton natans* and *Elodea canadensis*). I say to them, search and you shall find weed-free areas.

So I chose my rig, plumbed up carefully and found plenty of the aforementioned weed with a small clearing. This did not deter me, as I know how to deal with fishing in weed. A couple of small pouches of micro pellets went in first, followed by a small pot of maggots, about 20 in all (maggots that is, not pots). Two maggots were hooked onto a size 18 hook and out it went. An important aspect of fishing in and over weed is not to shot the float down too far.

Within a couple of minutes I got indications of fish in the area and the float told me I was straight into my first fish, a small common carp of about a pound. My no.8 elastic stretched out as I lifted into the fish, and as expected it made a dash for the Elodea weed, but it was no problem and soon came to the net. Straight back out again with two fresh maggots on the hook and almost immediately I was into another fish. It was the exact same reaction as the previous fish, only this one was a bit larger.

So about 15 minutes into the session it was looking good, I thought. Thirty minutes went by without any more indications, so I repeated the initial process and it wasn't long before I was into a string of mirrors. One after the other followed into the net with several commons coming in as well. With regular feeding of micro pellet and a few maggots, I was thinking this was too easy. Why people were complaining about poor fishing and being unable to catch was beyond me. It was a doddle.

About 12.30pm it went quite dark and the heavens opened. It was getting to that time when I was thinking about packing up, but I just wanted a couple more fish and didn't want to

pack up in the rain, so I stuck it out for another half hour, netting a further three fish. I finished the session when the rain stopped at 1.10pm and went on my way having landed about 15 carp, so I was quite chuffed.

I quite enjoy writing the blogs, they don't take up too much time and apart from anything else it is a record of some of my angling activities to look back on later. As I alluded to before, it doesn't matter to me if hordes of people around the world don't want to read them, but if anyone does and gets some kind of insight into my world of fishing then that will do for me.

CHAPTER 10

A New Direction –
Fly-fishing

I had thought about fly-fishing many years before while I was living in the south, but I was under the impression it was a sport solely for the wealthy, upper-class gentry of privileged circles. I knew of a few trout fisheries in West Sussex, but they all needed fat wallets to even contemplate joining the syndicates and to learn how to cast would be in itself a costly exercise. So it was something I never pursued until I looked into fly-fishing venues in Cheshire. Looking through an Environment Agency booklet of fisheries, I was pleasantly surprised to find several within a short distance of Stockport which were accessible to day-ticket anglers. And what's more, they didn't need a call to the bank manager for a loan. There were also a number of GAIA-qualified casting instructors associated with these fisheries. The opportunity was certainly there for me to seize the moment and try the sport.

Probably the most beneficial aspect of fly-fishing was it didn't involve humping huge amounts of tackle around trying to find a decent spot to fish. My wife indicated that she might like to have a go at fly-fishing as well and encouraged my interest in finding out more about the sport. Her interest was my cue to go out and buy some beginner's fly-fishing gear without further hesitation, so on the first available Sunday afternoon a trip to Stapely Angling Centre was arranged. On arrival we were greeted by an elderly gentleman who was extremely helpful and understanding towards a pair of middle-aged novices keen to learn as much as possible in the shortest time possible. I think the only thing we learned that day was that it was going to take a lot longer than we first thought to master this sport.

An hour or two later we set off for home satisfied with our purchase of a couple of Leeda fly-fishing outfits and a basic selection of dry and wet flies. I really had no idea what the flies were except the obvious Mayfly and Daddy Longlegs imitations, but I was sure to learn eventually. Once home, I booked a couple of hours' instruction for the two of us to learn how to cast and set up our equipment accordingly. It was the best 30 quid I have spent in all my angling years and I came away with the ability to cast a reasonable distance and a whole lot of knowledge about flies and nymphs. I suppose you could say that the seed was well and truly sown, with me at least. My wife also enjoyed her brief acquaintance with fly-fishing. Not surprisingly she didn't take to it with as much enthusiasm as me, but then not many do.

I literally hung up my coarse angling gear to concentrate on fly-fishing, leaving GOSJAC AC in the 2014/15 season having accomplished all I had set out to achieve. I suppose if the truth be known, what really made my mind up was when on a visit to Tara Lake at Cudmore Fishery in Staffordshire, I needed to make two trips to my peg from the van to carry all my gear. I just couldn't manage it all in one go. Even so, the enjoyment of coarse fishing will never leave me, and to this day I look forward to a day's trotting for grayling on the rivers.

I acknowledged that there was a lot for me to learn about fly-fishing and I threw myself in to it, learning as much as I could from books and the internet, but most of all from practising at any possible moment I could. The best of it was I could always put in a couple of hours on my local fishery at Mobberley, after, or sometimes during, my working day. It was no bother to put the gear in the van out of the way from my work gear. Another advantage was that whenever my wife and I took a trip away at a weekend the fishing gear didn't take up much room in the car and a couple of hours spent on a fishery anywhere in the country was always possible.

As my experience with trout fishing grew, I was persuaded to have a go at salmon fishing on the rivers of Scotland. Yet another angling discipline to learn and not only that, another new collection of fishing tackle was needed. Fortunately I was in a position to be able to buy a new salmon rod and reel as recommended to me by a friend, and a quick casting lesson from an instructor had me hooked on the hunt for the King of Fish, or the Silver Tourist as some anglers call them.

I knew an older gentleman with many years of experience in salmon fishing who was having to give up the sport due to failing health, and he wanted me to have some of his gear for a token price. He insisted that £75 was more than enough, a token price indeed, and refused to accept a higher offer from me, allowing me to take dozens of salmon flies, a spinning rod and reel, lures, spinners and all manner of accessories. In no time at all I had most of the gear but absolutely no idea. But that was all soon to change.

Since then I have not looked back, and my enjoyment and enthusiasm with fly-fishing, for both trout and salmon, remains with me to this day.

I had been fly-fishing for a few years before I had the pleasure of being introduced to young man called Kieran who was very keen on learning how to fly fish. Now I am no casting expert, but I can throw a line a good distance using the most common overhead and roll casts. I am, however, a dab hand at observation and watercraft, which to me are more important than being a fancy caster. I explained to Kieran and his father that if Kieran wanted to progress to learning the full art of the casting technique, then a GAIA casting instructor would be beneficial to him. Kieran is still with me after several years and is catching many, many fish, and I have featured him several times within my collaborative anthology.

I hope you enjoy reading about some of my experiences with fly-fishing and realise that there is much more to angling than catching fish.

A VISIT TO SCOTLAND

No matter how much time is spent on preparation for a fishing trip with checking equipment, booking venues, current river levels, booking accommodation, researching who's catching what, where and on which flies, you just cannot predict what the weather is going to be like at any given time, especially in the glens of Scotland. The weather forecast is all very well and can be very accurate with regards to your exact location occasionally, and in early June, you would expect a little bit of summer at some point.

Bev and I left home at 5 am one June Sunday morning in order to arrive at Glensherup trout fishery in the picturesque Glen Devon east of Stirling for 10 am, allowing for a short break for breakfast midway, at Gretna Services. The wind and rain kept me wide awake and alert for the entire journey – I was doing all the driving on this trip. There was very little traffic to play leapfrog with to ease the mesmerism of the monotonous rhythm and sound of the windscreen wipers.

Thankfully the time seemed to pass quickly enough and we arrived at the fishery at 9.45 am. At least it had stopped raining and the clouds were beginning to break, but the wind - oh that wind! It was blowing so hard up the loch that the surface was more like the sea, with 'white horses' crashing into the dam wall. There were a couple of boats out on the water, but it made me feel sea sick just looking at them, so as before, I opted to bank fish as I was only there for a couple of hours anyway.

The loch was full to capacity with a steady flow cascading down the burn to the River Devon. This was in stark contrast to my previous two visits when the level had been 10-12 feet down, revealing bands of shingle beaches and allowing the angler to easily negotiate with care the entire circumference of the 29-acre loch.

With this kind of depth in front of me I would have to use an extra-long leader of up to 20ft and three flies to find the fish, but in this wind, it would not be easy. The fishery manager invited me to use the floating boat pontoon, as there was no chance of casting from the only accessible bank, which was off the dam wall and faced directly into the wind. I did walk around just to see if it was feasible, but after three or four failed attempts I gave up. I returned to the boat moorings and ventured out onto the pontoon.

It was like trying to keep your balance on a bouncy castle, and when I finally reached the end it was a job for me to stay upright, but I soon got used to it and began to cast with the wind behind me. Boy was I reaching good distances with my cast, with very little effort. It went so far away I couldn't see the indicator I was using above my two buzzers, so I changed it to a blob just in case an inquisitive fish wanted to have a go, which a couple did, but I missed them both. It seemed the fish were not down too deep despite the recent rain, so so I shortened my leader for ease of casting. Even then I had no interest at all on the buzzers and I was starting to think I could draw a blank today. I only saw one fish being caught by seven anglers in the four boats that by now were out in the middle bobbing up and down.

The sun was at last breaking through the dispersing cloud, and in a last-ditch attempt to catch a fish I changed to a Klinkhamer. As if on cue a fish rose to my left near the bank. I cast over it and almost immediately it snatched at the fly, but I didn't connect and missed the take. A second cast to the same spot induced another take, and this time I made a good connection and the fish immediately dived to deeper water, taking line with it. It felt a good fish. The fight went on for ages and the fish just didn't want come up. A boat came in behind me with two anglers on board and the usual angling banter began, tinged with Scottish accents, which amused me whilst I was still fighting the fish.

After a further few minutes the fish finally gave up and came to the net. It was a nice fish of about 3lb but it had fought like a monster and my new friends confirmed that the fish in there do put up a good scrap pound for pound.

A short while afterwards I decided I had had enough battling against the wind and a well-earned brew was beckoning. I was thinking of Bev, who had been sitting in the van all this time. We both called into the cabin and engaged in further banter with the local anglers, who made us very welcome, and it was a pleasure to accompany them as they had their coffee and biscuits. Almost an hour passed and it was time to say our farewells, so we thanked them for their hospitality and I assured them that I would return on my next trip to Scotland.

After a very filling lunch at Tormaukin Hotel in Glen Devon, our journey continued toward Montrose, terminating at the Marykirk Hotel, where we would be staying for three nights. After checking in I was keen to find the Gallery Beat on the River North Esk. This was to be my salmon-fishing venue for the next two days. Up and down the lane we drove, but we couldn't find any signs directing us to the beat, so we gave up and decided to wait until the morning, when I would obtain directions from the fishery manager.

At breakfast the next morning I started up a conversation with two guys called Hugh and Glen, discovering that they were on one of their regular trips to the North Esk, and indeed they were going to fish the Gallery Beat alongside me. After a superb Scottish breakfast I followed them to the river and was introduced to the beat's manager, Neil Anderson.

The river was running low and gin clear, so Neil's advice was for me to use a floating line with a clear slow sinking tip and small fly, preferably a Stoat's Tail. Fortunately I had several of these flies and was soon tackled up and raring to go. Neil took me to the nearest pool, which is appropriately named Gallery, and advised me on how to fish this pool. The weather was unrelenting with high winds and occasional blustery showers, more like the weather we are used to in November. However, I was togged up as if for the winter with thermal underpants beneath my chest waders, fleece and waterproof wading jacket.

Casting across within 12 inches of the far bank as instructed by Neil proved difficult for me at first. Neil had a good laugh at my technique, not sure whether I was Spey casting or roll casting. I always get nervous when I have an experienced angler looking on, especially when the said angler fishes for the national team. He wasn't there to coach me and left me to improve on my technique alone. My technique did improve with practice and I was regularly hitting the desired spot.

After a couple of casts I had my first pull on the line, and my heart missed a beat. That gave me huge amounts of confidence, and my casting became perfect every time in spite of the blustery conditions. It wasn't long before I was into my first fish of the day, but it wasn't what I hoped for, just a very small smolt on its migration down to the sea.

But where there are small ones, there have to be bigger
ones – well that's what I kept telling myself. Although it
certainly is fantastic to see them, the novelty of catching
these little fish soon wore off, specially as in between the
smolts I was also catching even smaller parr further down
the pool.

Although I didn't connect with a proper salmon, I did get
the pleasure of seeing one swimming towards me on its
way upstream. It almost swam through my legs as I stood
motionless watching its movements. It was my first-ever
sighting of a female salmon and was so close I could have
touched its fin to wish it well for its onward journey up the
glen to spawn.

After I had been fishing for an hour, Neil returned to take
me to the lowest pool of the beat, named Cobbleheugh (river
crossing), which lay in the shadows of an arched railway

bridge. Again he advised me where the fish generally rested up and the best places to put my cast. I cast a few times before hitting the spot as per instruction. Neil was right, as a fish soon took my fly near the rocks and leapt from the water, throwing the hook. I wasn't sure whether it was a salmon or a sea trout, but either way it was a proper fish and once again it gave me a huge confidence boost.

Neil then guided me to a narrow run, hard up against one of the bridge stanchions. My cast had to be some way upstream so my fly would naturally flow into the exact spot where he had previously seen a flash from a fish near the stony bottom of the glide, but he couldn't be certain if it was a salmon or sea trout. Getting the cast into the right position for the current to present the fly to the fish took me about three casts, and then – wham! – I felt the tug of a fish taking my fly and moments later I was into the fish. This time it was hooked properly and the fight was on.

It was clearly a sea trout as it leapt clear of the water, but I wasn't going to let this one go. Holding the rod high, I soon had the fish under control and steered it toward the waiting landing net, where Neil scooped it up with precision.

So my first-ever proper North Esk fish was in the net, a perfectly clean silver 3lb sea trout. I was chuffed to bits and thanked Neil for his skilled observations, but I still wanted that elusive Atlantic salmon.

After returning the fish to continue its journey, we left the pool and returned to the cabin for lunch. Hugh and Glen were already tucking into their sandwiches but had had no luck at all in catching a fish. I must admit to a little gloating – well, it was my first time. I proudly noted the fish down in the catch return book.

After lunch I returned to the river, as advised by Neil, to try the Laird's Cast pool. The weather was getting worse, with showers of rain lashing down in the driving wind, but that didn't deter me as I was on a high. Hugh and Glen stayed put in the cosy cabin for a sleep.

The Laird's Cast is a long fast-flowing section that has deep runs close in to the near bank with rocks and boulders for the fish to rest behind, but if I could see them (which I couldn't) then they could see me. I hadn't seen a salmon all day, but now I noticed a small one running in the fast open water. It was only three or four pounds, and it was on a mission. He or she wasn't going to stop for anyone or anything, so I let it be and worked my way down the pool, catching one or two more smolt and parr.

So that was my first day. I packed away at 5 pm and headed back to the hotel, leaving Hugh and Glen to sit it out for better weather for the later sea trout run in the evening. However, during the evening the weather turned even worse and it rained and rained. Hugh and Glen soon returned to the hotel with noticeably saddened expressions on their faces, having blanked. The only saving grace was that we could all drown our sorrows over a few beers and a wee dram. At last this was an activity Bev could join in with, and we all had a pleasant evening.

All night the rain came down and the prospects of a good day's fishing the next day went down the drain with the rainwater as it cascaded down the road, which by now was more akin to the river. But whatever the weather, I was determined to endeavour.

We all met Neil at 9am and he reaffirmed our fears of poor prospects, as the river had risen two feet overnight and was running chocolate brown. Different rigs and lines would be required to tackle this kind of flow, so Neil advised an extra-fast sink tip with a much larger fly – something like a Monkey with plenty of colour would probably be best. I cast and I cast and I cast until my arms ached; all morning I cast, but nothing. Hugh and Glen gave up as the wind was getting far too strong for them, so they went back to the cabin at lunch time, lit the wood-burning fire and fell asleep for the afternoon on the warm comfy leatherette sofas. But I wasn't having any of that. As the sky brightened, I ventured back downstream to the bridge at Cobbleheugh to find a totally different landscape fromn the day before. Having been able to walk out to the rocks without getting a wet foot the previous day, wading was the only way to reach the same spot where I had caught the sea trout.

Once I had gingerly made my way out to the rocks I made several casts, to no avail. It was clearly a futile exercise and a waste of effort. In my book I never say never, but although the river had dropped a few inches and was fining down, it wasn't to be. Perhaps it would fish better later into the evening. I wasn't going to stay, but Hugh and Glen did. At breakfast the next morning they confirmed that they had stayed until 11pm without a take.

After another wonderful breakfast we said our goodbyes and thanked each other for the company. Even though the fishing wasn't terrific it was an enjoyable couple of days, and I confirmed that I would return, whatever the weather.

On our way home Bev and I called into Bessy Beck Trout Fishery south of Penrith in Cumbria for a couple of hours. The sun was shining and the wind was still howling, but at least there was no sign of rain. I fished the Island pool, as it was the only pool where they offered catch and release, and in those two hours I had six rainbows to 6½ lb. So that was a pleasing end to a thoroughly enjoyable few days.

Bev didn't have the same views on the trip as me, as she did get a little bored with sitting in the van all the time I was fishing, but at least she did get a good rest from work and we had a good laugh and met some new acquaintances, an added bonus in angling, and what it's all about.

CHAPTER 11

A Little More Local

I found myself leaning over a road bridge, as we anglers do, and putting on my polarised sunglasses to get a clearer view of the aquatic life below the surface of this medium-paced river. Only 3 metres wide at most, it snaked through meadows less than 200 metres from rural village life. The crystal-clear water revealed the stone and shingle bed above which fronds of streamer weed waved in the current. In the shallower riffles, great clumps of Ranunculi formed blankets of green, white and yellow, providing sanctuary for all kinds of insects and invertebrates.

I spotted the unmistakeable dark silhouettes of small fish darting between midstream rocks and tree roots reaching out from the banks below and above the surface. Some of these banks were as high as five feet above the water, while others just gently sloped down to the water's edge from the undulating contours of the adjacent fields.

Then I spotted my quarry – a wild brown trout about 12 feet from where I was standing on the bridge. I would guess it was 10 inches long, and it hung as though it was suspended midwater from invisible cords in the gentle current, occasionally making sideway movements to take nymphs or other food morsels that drifted down within easy reach, saving him from expending too much energy. His feeding station was under a high nearside bank which had been undercut by the current, making for a difficult cast for even the most accomplished angler, let alone me. The only way was to creep up out of sight and plop a nymph upstream, then let it drift down with the current and feel for any tug on the line that would indicate a take.

I slowly moved from my viewing point on the bridge and crawled to the bank edge as close as I dared. Then I lay flat on my front, gingerly placing my rod over the water to obtain an angle in readiness to let go of the line and let my nymphs drift down to where I thought the trout was feeding. I was using a beaded nymph as a dropper to get close to the stony river bed and a smaller, lighter Hare's Ear nymph on the point which should appear quite natural. The pain from a large stone hidden under the grass which pressing itself into my stomach was excruciating. I twisted to one side to ease the pain and the wrist of my rod arm stroked against some nettles, delivering that unmistakable stinging twinge all the way up to my elbow. I swore to myself, grimacing in discomfort.

I looked up to the sky and was immediately distracted by two walkers dressed in hi-viz fluorescent orange and pink cagoules leaning over the bridge, as I had just done. One called, "Have you caught anything yet?" I grunted and muttered, "Well, I'm not going to catch anything now," and made a swift retreat, cursing their intrusion of my fishing space under my breath.

Gathering myself together, I decided to leave this swim

for later, assuming the fish would surely have been spooked into taking cover or heading off upstream. This was my first visit to this little river, so I had no idea what I would find around the corner. My main task was to find likely places where trout might be lurking for future visits. I found fast-flowing shallow glides and slower, deep pools on the bends formed by the winter floods eroding the banks away over the decades. The water was less clear in these areas and it was very likely large fish could be living under the overhanging bushes and trees.

It was a balmy summer's evening and the sun was losing its strength as it began to sink behind the trees. Swarms of midges danced above the river in their seemingly choreographed mating ritual just before dusk. A small fish rose within easy casting range to take a midge as it landed on the water surface. I settled down to change my leader and tied on a small CDC emerger, then cast nicely above the area of the rise, but there was no response. Again and again I cast, but nothing happened. I knew there was a fish there, so why didn't he want my fly? Maybe it was the wrong size, maybe it was the wrong colour or maybe it was too low in the surface film – or maybe even he could see my tippet; I couldn't!

I decided to try a small Klinkhamer, the smallest I had, so I degreased my tippet with imitation mud and cast again. Eureka! The fish took my fly and torpedoed downwards to the river bed in a bid to seek sanctuary amongst the tree roots. I exerted pressure on the line and held him away from reaching his lair, and after a sprightly fight, this small fish came to my waiting hand and I rested him on the damp grass.

I never tire of catching little beauties like this, although obviously it is also nice to catch larger specimens, but I believe angling is more about how and where the fish are caught rather than about the size.

I retired from that swim and wandered off in the hope of finding more delights further upstream. There were lots of potential areas where fish might be resident, but I soon came to the end of the beat. An hour had passed and the sun was now behind the trees, so I wasted no time in returning to the bridge for a final stab at the fish I had spotted earlier. On reaching the bridge I peered over towards where the fish had been lying, but I couldn't see it this time.

Nonetheless I was going to try again. Changing back to my duo nymph setup, I resumed my previous posture, this time remembering where the hidden stone was and keeping well away from those pesky stinging nettles. All went well as I managed to drop the nymphs in the right place and fed line out from the reel, teasing the nymphs along the bottom.

Almost immediately I felt a pull and struck into a fish. I quickly got to my knees and played the fish to the waiting net. Sounds easy, but netting a fish on the end of a very flexible rod while leaning over a bank that has a drop of four feet to the water is not funny, although it might seem hilarious to anyone else watching. But I managed it and this stunning wild brownie was mine. Not huge by any means, but a beautiful creature and a privilege to make its acquaintance.

There was no way I was going to attempt a release where I had caught him due to the long drop to the water, but after a short walk downstream, I managed to slide down the bank and gently release him where he would easily find his way back home. While I was standing in the river I thought I would take another photo of a potential glide that I planned to try on a return visit. What an enjoyable couple of hours I had had.

So where is this little river? Is it a carrier of the River Test or Itchen or some other iconic chalk stream in the south of England? No, it's the River Dean near Bollington, Cheshire!

IN SEARCH OF SALMON AND GRAYLING
ON THE WELSH DEE

I checked in to my accommodation early afternoon on the Sunday afternoon in Clocaenog near Ruthin, my base for the week. The necessary unloading of domestic accessories from the van was hastily undertaken in earnest, so I could get down to the river for a quick look at some of the prospective beats and maybe a cast or two if time allowed. Armed with my rule book and maps, I headed towards the Berwyn Arms section and the Bridge Pool.

Parking at the road junction, I walked down to the bridge and found the river to be in near perfect condition for me, as a newcomer to the Dee. I noticed a disused access pathway adjacent to the bridge and thought I could easily get down the bank about 30 feet below. The first 10 feet was easy, but then my body soon wanted to go faster than my little legs would carry it and my descending speed soon became faster, until I could no longer stop. I began to think my decision to try to get in at this point was a huge mistake, because then I noticed a fallen bough blocking my final escape route to the field below. I crashed through the branches with arms and legs flying around in the air like a spider in a spin dryer, and finally came to a standstill several yards from the embankment.

Whilst miraculously still on my feet I gathered myself together, but I had realised that I was not 21 any more and should not be taking such foolhardy risks. The horrendous commotion I had made disturbed an angler who promptly appeared from his casting station and calmly said in a strong Welsh accent, "Are you OK, boyo?" Half laughing and half wincing from pain, I answered that I was and assured him I would not be doing that again. Having gained some invaluable information from him about the fishing in this pool, I left him to it and returned to the van via the field gate not 20 yards away.

My next stop was Chain Pool, where I found two anglers who were about to leave, and they kindly provided me with some tips on where to put my fly. They both suggested that I should have a cast, as they confirmed that there were some fish in the pool even though they had failed to catch themselves. It didn't take much persuasion, and I was soon tackled up and raring to have my very first cast on the Welsh Dee. One of the guys joined me, but neither of us had a take.

The next morning after a sleepless night (excitement kept me awake), I arrived at Chain Pool once more, armed with my 14ft salmon rod, to see a stunning sunrise over the Dee valley.

I fished the pool through twice without seeing a salmon, so I moved onto the Bridge Pool, where I had made my not-so-elegant debut the previous afternoon. Again, I fished without success, so I moved on to explore a beat named The Run. Exploring was going to be the primary approach for the week as I had never seen any of the beats before and had nobody to introduce me to them. Eventually I found my way to the beat and ran a fly through the top section, learning about the water and its characteristics without any sight of a salmon.

I returned to Chain Pool, where I met up with another member who suggested I tried running a spinner through, as this method had produced fish throughout the season. Searching through my kit bag I found no sign of my Flying Cs, spinners, lures or accessories, only a selection of Blair spoons and Tobies were in the bag. I could only think that I must have left them on the bank in Scotland at the beginning of the summer. The frustration was not only over the cost of replacing them all but the fact that the lack of accessories meant I could not even use my spoons or Tobies. A trip to the local tackle shop was going to be a priority in the morning.

The next morning, an early fly session on Chain Pool before making a visit to the tackle shop in Corwen proved fruitless. About an hour later I resurfaced from this Aladdin's cave very pleased with my purchases of much more gear than I had imagined I needed. I felt I was now equipped with spinners, lures and accessories to last a lifetime. Returning to the Bridge Pool I put my new Flying Cs into action, but

with no luck again, so I ventured off to find out about the renowned Taylor's Pool.

This was lovely fly water and easy to fish, but alas I couldn't find any salmon. The day soon passed and I wanted another thrash at Chain Pool on my return to "base camp". I changed my Cascade fly to a smaller version that I had bought earlier in the day, and although I still couldn't tempt a salmon this little wild brownie couldn't resist it. For its size it put up a good fight.

A little sigh of relief came over me, for at least I hadn't drawn another blank day.

The following day I decided I would have a break from the river and visit a still water that I had learned about, Graiglwyd Springs Fishery near Llandudno; ha ha ha! I arrived soon after 8:15 and the place was almost full. I paid my fees and stayed for less than five minutes without having a cast. It was like a circus, crowded with people with little angling skill pulling out fish everywhere. It was obviously overstocked with fresh fish that would take anything. This place was not for me. I got my money back and headed back to the river.

I thought I would try the upper beats for a change and drove off to the lower end of Crogen 2, where I met another member, who was finishing his session with a blank. He advised me not to bother, but said I should try the top end of Beat 1. I was unsure of the exact location, but he offered to lead me there and show me where to fish. From the access point it was a good walk to the top of the beat, but he assured me it would be worth it. I agreed and after a short drive we arrived at the estate house and the gentleman showed me where to go.

I was told had to walk across all the fields and around the corner, where I would find the beat limit sign, and it was there I should try for a salmon. Off I set on my country hike armed with my salmon rod, and about 20 minutes later I arrived at this lovely-looking pool.

The river was running low, but there was a deeper and faster channel on the far side. I edged my way across to the middle and began to cast and make my way down the pool. As I reached a deeper section I stopped and peered into the water. The light was at a perfect angle and I could clearly see the bottom with my polarised glasses. What I could see fascinated me, and I stopped fishing and just gazed into the flow. I could see fish-shaped silhouettes moving in and out with the current around my feet. They were grayling feeding on the grubs and nymphs that I was disturbing from the river bed. Some were of decent size and were not spooked in any way by my presence.

I moved downstream, still casting for salmon, but saw nothing. There was no doubt in my mind that the next morning I would return with my grayling gear. Filled with renewed excitement I returned to the van and went off for a return visit to the Run, where I not unexpectedly blanked again.

An early morning rise saw me back at the Crogen 2

beat again armed with my grayling rod and nymphs. My expectations of catching a few were high. I ventured out to the middle of the river just below the island, where I began to run the nymphs through, adjusting my leader length as and when required.

Halfway down the pool I found the fish where I had seen them the day before, and soon I became attached to one grayling after another. Several fish came to the net and they were all like peas in a pod, ranging from 12oz to over a pound in weight, but nothing like the specimens I had been told were present. However, I was pleased with my morning's work and decided to return the following morning. I returned for the afternoon to Chain Pool and Bridge Pool in search of salmon, but once again there was nothing and I blanked again.

I repeated my expedition to Crogan 2 on my final day on the Dee and once again the grayling didn't disappoint and had several more, but not as many as the previous day. Perhaps word had got out in the fishy world that something was not quite right and they had gone into hiding. For my last cast I would return to Chain Pool, but further up the beat this time searching for grayling. However I could only find a small brownie.

This was to be my last fish of the week. I called halt to my visit a day early and headed back to base for the final time. It had been a great week on the Dee, and I had learned a lot about the river. I looked forward to returning later in the season for more grayling sessions.

I have mixed feelings about the salmon fishing as my opportunities available to me may not be frequent enough. I heard that salmon were caught during the week, but I didn't see one and none of the members I had met had had one, but they are there, so I will keep searching.

"OI YOU! STOP USING INDICATORS!"

There we were, Kieran and I, setting up our rods in preparation for another session at Mobberley, leisurely sipping at a cup of coffee and pondering over what flies would most likely work, when along came Brian the owner, in his old jalopy of a Jeep. He was puffing away on a ciggy (probably a Woodbine) and mumbling away to himself. "I hope you haven't been smoking in that cabin" I sternly enquired, "otherwise I'll have to inform the boss" (his wife Margret) I said. The sweet sound of @#~%!/*? was his instant retort, making Kieran and me laugh. "What's that you're using?" he asked, nodding at my rod with a disapproving expression. I had just tied an Orange Blob onto my line with a buzzer four feet down on the point. "Indicators are banned," he reminded me.

"I know that, that's why I'm using a Blob fly" I replied. He drove off, leaving Kieran and me to get on. Kieran decided he wanted to try a small lure on his rod, while I set up a second rod with a mini Cat's Whisker. These small lures still work at this time of year in early spring, but seemingly only first thing in the morning – after that the fish tend to switch right off them.

The weather was fine with strong, gusting winds and the possibility of a few showers later on in the day, so not a bad day for fly-fishing, taking into account the awkwardness of the wind. Normally I would have a dabble on the way down to the bottom end of the lake, but I thought I would stay close to Kieran, thinking he might have difficulty casting in the facing wind.

The first couple of casts brought some tentative enquiries

from fish, but nothing to hook up with. Kieran was actually casting well, but he was leaving the back cast too long and the leader was clipping the hedge behind. Eventually one of his back casts got securely hung up in the bushes and his leader snapped on the forward cast. He came over to me for a replacement. I had just cast out, so I handed him my rod to retrieve the line whilst I sorted his tackle out. As sure as god made little apples, he went and latched on to a fish. It was a good fish as well and took line off the spool, and I couldn't believe it could happen yet again. Time and time again I have handed him my rod for a few moments and he has repayed my good nature by catching a fish.

I stopped what I was doing and fetched the camera as I could see this seemed a nice fish. Kieran played the fish well and soon landed this 4lb Rainbow.

He had a smug look on his face and was gloating from ear to ear, well pleased with himself. It took me a while to get over the cheek of it. Not only that, the fish had trashed my lure in the fight and rendered it useless, so in the bin it was destined to go, and to rub salt in the wound, it was my last one of that pattern. Huh!

It was time for the Blob and buzzer duo set up. Almost immediately fish were coming to the Blob and either scooping it from the surface or taking the buzzer suspended below. I caught three fish in about half an hour, which put a smile on my face. I suggested Kieran should switch to this method, as there had been a lack of interest in the lure he was using. I made him up a set-up identical to mine and sure enough he was getting some interest but missing the fish on the strike.

A little instruction from me soon had him landing his first fish of the day on the buzzer, but the wind began to get the better of him and the two flies became entangled in each other, so a new rig was needed. I decided we should move around the pool to the middle section, where there were several fish about 15 metres out and in easy casting reach. It was also a little less windy, and certainly wasn't swirling as it was at the end of the pool. I soon had another couple of fish on the Blob. The fish here seemed uninterested in the buzzer, but they were attacking the Blob like nothing I had witnessed before. Kieran was in the adjacent peg and striking away but missing the takes. It was pandemonium for a while, until in the excitement Kieran managed to get into another tangle. Again I handed him my rod while I changed his leader, and blow me down if he didn't get another fish first cast.

Just then Brian returned behind us and bellowed from his Jeep across the hedge, "Oi you! Stop using indicators!" I reminded him that we were using the Blob fly and the fish were going crazy over it. Quite bemused, he watched as I cast out again and straight away a fish jumped onto the Blob and took off, leaping two feet out of the water and stripping line off the reel.

"How many have you had now?" he asked.

"I don't know. I've lost count."

"Those Blobs are banned," he said.

"There's nothing to say that in the cabin," I replied.

"Well they are from now," he quickly asserted.

DECEMBER IS A GREAT TIME FOR FISHING

I thought somewhere different would be good, so I decided to visit a fishery near Bolton and asked my friend Steve Millington, or Millie as he is better known, if he wanted to come too. So there we were on this cold and frosty morning contemplating a large volume of water that neither of us had been to before, with nobody there to ask for information on the best flies or areas to fish or even how deep the water was.

We chose to try the pontoons first, as they were sheltered from the cold wind blowing from the north and Millie went for a sinking line and lures whilst I chose a floating line with long leader and a team of three buzzers.

Millie had his back to me on the adjacent pontoon as he was thrashing about with his lure, so he was quite oblivious to my gentle flicking out of the buzzers. I received a little interest from a passing fish but nothing to strike at. I changed the top dropper and put on an indicator and on the second cast I had a proper take and the indicator sailed away as I struck into a nice fish. Following a feisty fight, this fin-perfect rainbow came to the net. It had taken the middle dropper about 4 feet below the indicator.

Not long after that a second take resulted in another
rainbow of similar size and quality, but this one had taken
the point buzzer about 8 feet below the indicator. Millie was
still trying his luck with the lure but had not received any
interest from a fish whatsoever. It was time for a brew and a
breakfast bap from the café.

We returned to the same area after our break, but neither
of us received any indication of fish in the vicinity for the two
hours we stayed until we were packing up, when a fish came
to the surface right in front of me as if to say ha ha ha, he he
he, here I am and you couldn't catch me.

The following day it was an early start to get to the river
Dee at Corwen before dawn. I invited Millie as my guest for
the day and our first beat was going to be Crogen 2. It was
pretty cold in Stockport as we left at 6:30, and the temperature
plummeted further as we arrived at our destination.

Wondering what fools would be out fishing in these temperatures, we made light of the situation and tackled up. It didn't take long for our fingertips to get numb with the cold, but the thought that the river water would be warmer than the air spurred us on as we marched off to find the start of the beat across the fields. I had fished this beat in early October and had caught several grayling here, but that didn't mean we would find some today as they shoal up in deeper water at this time of year.

By the time we eventually arrived we had warmed up nicely from the hike, and began fishing. The scenery was stunning, as every blade of grass and tree branch was covered in frost and steam was rising from the warmer water of the river. I couldn't resist taking a photo.

I set Millie off first and then I followed on behind searching for our quarry, but nothing seemed to be there, or at least if they were, they weren't interested in our flies. We both passed through the pool a second time with nothing to

show and after a couple of hours up to our crotches in cold water we decided it was time for a warm up at Yum Yum's Café in Corwen. We smiled at three elderly ladies who were giving us bewildered looks as we tucked into our coffee and breakfast baps dressed in waders, boots, thermal jackets and woolly hats.

Suitably refreshed and a great deal warmer, we headed off to the Town Waters, a stretch I hadn't fished before. It was by now less cold at a mere -4 degrees as we set off downstream from the road bridge. I began in the deeper waters before the river shallowed off to where Millie was fishing on the corner. Standing up to my waist in almost freezing water was not the best idea I've ever had. I didn't stick it out too long and soon ventured down to see Millie – just as he hooked his first fish. Well – it was a fish, a very cute current year's fingerling of a grayling. Small maybe, but perfectly formed – now I've heard that somewhere before!

Where there are small ones there must be bigger ones, and as Millie moved downstream he became attached to one. His first ever "proper" grayling was caught in the almost static water of a back eddy, the most unlikely place you'd think of catching a grayling.

The camera angle doesn't do the fish justice (nor Millie for that matter, in his wife's furry hat) - we estimated it to be not far short of 2lb and quite a specimen.

I blanked once again on this beat, so we moved further downstream to just above Chain Pool, a nice straight even run, and very easy to fish. Off we two intrepid piscators trudged across the field with a renewed spring in our steps, now feeling extra positive as the temperature had risen to zero. It wasn't long before

I followed Millie with another fingerling grayling, although it was slightly bigger. Then I got into a proper fish, though it

was not as big as Millie's specimen. It was a lively grayling
of around 1¼ lb.

The two of us were now even, although weight-wise Millie
was easily ahead as we moved on to our final beat of the day.
The Bridge Pool at Berwyn Arms brought back memories of
my slightly less elegant introduction to the Dee a few months
previously. It seemed to be even colder down in the valley, as
what little sun there was couldn't find its way through the
trees, so we didn't spend much time here before deciding to
call it a day. And what a day it was – thoroughly enjoyable
despite the cold and well worth the journey, even though we
only caught four fish between us.

Our final fling before New Year was back to "The Office"
at Mobberley. Millie, Ray and I had arranged the day and no
doubt Brian would make a showing as well, especially if he
knew there were doughnuts to be scoffed.

On my way I called in to the Co-op to buy doughnuts, but alas there were none of the sort we like, so I was compelled to purchase chocolate brownie bites, iced Belgian buns and glazed ring doughnuts. Millie arrived armed with two boxes of mince pies and Ray somehow managed to get two bags of custard and jam doughnuts from his local Co-op. With coffee and tea provided, this fodder had the makings of a belated Christmas party, and sure enough it wasn't long before Brian smelled the brewing coffee with all the sugary delights on offer and made his appearance.

More time was spent in the warm cabin stuffing our faces and talking man talk than was spent on the bank fishing, but when we did venture out things did not go to plan for either Millie or me. With excessively high blood sugar levels from the consumption of too many sugary delights our casting was not up to scratch, and we both ended up with several casts in the hedge behind us.

Eventually Millie managed to catch a couple in the middle of the pool, but then things went quiet, so I ventured off to the house end, where I soon began picking off several fish using my new 11ft #4 grayling nymphing rod. It was great fun playing the trout on this rod, but it was a little too soft and failed to get a good hookhold on several takes on the buzzer. However I did manage to land five. Uncharacteristically for Ray, he was struggling to connect with anything and had only managed one fish by the time I bade my farewells and seasonal greetings to everyone.

A BIRD IN THE HAND...

We arrived at Mobberley a little later than usual, and Kieran was eager to get cracking with his favourite Cat's Whisker and then move onto the Blob and buzzer method. He was beginning to understand that for the purist fly fisher the method is not strictly traditional fly-fishing, but it is a method that catches a lot of fish and is perfectly legal and ethical.

Whilst we were tackling up Brian, the owner, pootled up in his rusty but trusty old jalopy of a Jeep and immediately asked how I got on with my trip to the North Esk in Scotland. Why he needed reminding I don't know, because he'd been on the phone to me every day whilst I was standing in the river and I had given him a full update on the lack of fish each time.

Kieran was off to the house end of the pool, where he had seen a couple of fish mooching about earlier. He has picked up on the idea that if you want an early fish you have to search for them and take them before they know anyone is about. He has seen me do this several times and is learning the tactical approach to angling rather than just chucking and chancing.

Generally, lures cease to work well at this time of year, but as the night temperatures are still low at the moment and there is little natural fly activity in the first half of the morning, a small lure is always worth having a go with. This proved the case, as Kieran's second cast was picked up by a fish and he soon landed his first fish of the day. Several more fish fell to us both during the course of the morning, and Kieran had two fish in his bag to take home.

But there is always something special about early summer fishing out in the rural English countryside. Whilst I was retrieving a cast I was quite startled by something falling from the sky and landing in the grasses in front of me near the water edge. As I peered over I noticed this little fellow looking up at me. I'm not sure who was more confused as to what was going on.

It was a blue tit fledgling that had obviously taken its first flight from the nest and crash-landed before me. I reached over, and it quite happily jumped on to my hand and I lifted it to safety. It then fluttered up on to my fishing vest pocket, looked at me, chirped and then flew off into the hedgerow. How cute was that!

Mike Fox

NEVER MIND THE FISH, MORE CHOCOLATE BISCUITS PLEASE!

It is moments of peace and tranquillity like that shown in the above picture that put ideal angling conditions into second place in the importance scale. Kieran and I were greeted with these conditions on our arrival at Mobberley one Saturday morning. It was absolutely stunning, with the water surface reflecting the trees and sky like a mirror. Not exactly good angling conditions, but it was worth a few minutes to sit and enjoy such a view, with a cloud formation resembling snow-covered mountains in the distant background. The crystal-clear waters of the pool gave up its secrets, the deep holes and weed banks that were usually hidden from view. Fish in the upper levels of the water were making themselves all too obvious as they cruised around searching for hatching aquatic insects, occasionally breaking the surface to take an emerging buzzer. It was a totally idyllic world, and one we felt privileged to be part of.

The fishing for me was less important, but Kieran was his usual eager self, keen to set his rods up in anticipation of netting a few of those unsuspecting trout.

Buzzer and CDC Emergers were once again going to be the flies today, but with the still water and no wind whatsoever, presentation would be critical. I was the first to net a small Rainbow on a Grey Klinkhamer soon after we began casting, so straight away I tied a similar fly on to Kieran's 10ft monofilament leader. On his second cast he latched onto his first fish. Breaking the surface, it sent ripples across the formerly flat calm water.

The unusually flat conditions brought the kiss of death thereafter, and that was all we had to show in four hours of fishing, likewise for the other anglers who by now had joined us and were struggling to net a single fish between them. However, the disappointing fishing circumstances were joyfully put behind us during the traditional mid-morning coffee break, when we were accompanied by our fellow anglers in the cabin and of course the boss himself. Doughnuts and biscuits were woofed down with a fresh brew amid nonstop jibes from all corners about the less than clean accommodation. Kieran was a little unsure about this in the early days, but he has got used to this nonsensical banter now and happily joins in the fun. One thing we all agree on is that there are never enough chocolate biscuits in a packet when Brian's about.

CHAPTER 12

A Typical Year in Fly-Fishing

JANUARY

January can be a month of unpredictable angling weather and a time when some anglers pack their gear away, hang up their rods and wait for warmer days ahead. But for those willing to brave conditions that would see most sensible people snuggling up on the couch in front of a roaring fire, January can be a most rewarding month of the year.

Despite a fruitless trip to the river Dee at Corwen, when temperatures dropped to -4 with a prevailing bitter cold wind from the east, forcing me to cut short the one and only river session of the month with a blank, the fishing at Clay Lane Mobberley was remarkably productive. The buzzer hatches were few and far between, dry fly was out of the question and lures were hit or miss, as the fish had seen them all before. Something different was required, something that I knew had not been used to any extent on this water.

I had been tying a variety of flies for the coming spring season and decided to try out a corixa. Not at all in season, but I thought it worth a go. On my first visit of the month to Clay Lane I saw several fish showing in the middle of the pool and an easy roll cast with a slow retrieve saw me put my fly on the button. A 12 ft fluorocarbon leader would provide perfect presentation with very little surface disturbance.

Allowing the Corixa to sink 3-4ft, I lifted the rod to draw the fly back with a slow figure of eight retrieve, bringing the imitation bug through the water column in as natural a way as possible, and on the very first cast the tactic brought an instant result. A perfect rainbow soon came to the net following a feisty fight. They certainly do put up a scrap this time of year. A couple more fish soon followed the first and then it went quiet, so a change was needed.

Amongst the variety of flies I had been tying recently was the Squirmy Wormy, not exactly a fly, but who cares – I thought I would give it a go anyway. I had never tried the worm before so this would be a first for me. There is a lot of controversy regarding this fly, as many people do not regard using it as fly-fishing. My view is that if it is an imitation of natural fish food, then what is wrong with it? We use all kinds of imitative flies, so why not imitate a worm?

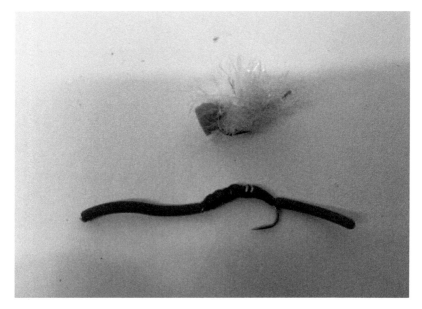

The red Squirmy Wormy and FAB (foam-arsed blob)

Having tied a Squirmy on to the leader I thought about freelining it along the bottom, but I knew there was quite a lot of filamentous weed spread over much of the lower levels of the water, so I tied on an FAB to use as a depth gauge and as a strike indicator. Standard indicators are for some reason banned here. It was an instant success, with fish coming to the net every half a dozen or so casts. When it eventually went quiet, I would move on to another area where fish were likely to have backed off, and the reaction was the same.

Even the poorest quality fish were finding the
Squirmy irresistible.

I was wondering if this reaction was a one off. Perhaps it was because the conditions were right and I was lucky in hitting the fish at the right time and in the right place. I decided to use this method again on a return visit.

A week later I returned and set up again the same outfit. I ventured off down the pool, casting in several areas and catching almost everywhere I cast to. Even close in by the reeds I found fish willing to take the worm. The weather conditions were certainly not the reason for catching, as they were totally different from those of the previous visits.

A third visit followed, and again I set up the same outfit. Once again the fish were hitting the worm with force, and some were taking the worm on the drop. I noticed that the fish that were taking it on the drop were deeply hooked and needed forceps to remove the hook, while those that took the worm on the indicator were hooked in the top lip. In most of these instances the barbless hook was self-released while the fish was still in the landing net.

I was by now receiving a lot of interest from other anglers as to what I was using and indeed similar inquisitiveness from the owners and it wasn't long before the muttering began and that I was accused of not using a "proper" fly-fishing method and that it was not "fair on the others".

During my most recent visit I was approached by the owner, who commented that the Blob was now banned on the fishery as I was using it as an indicator, and that indicators were banned in all other cases. I had landed seven fish in less than two hours and had missed many takes and lost (released at distance) several others. So I heeded the warning of being banned myself if I didn't change my tactics, and remove the Blob.

I was also reminded that fish welfare was of the utmost importance and that all anglers should respect fishery rules. I carried on freelining the Worm, catching a further four fish. They were all deeply hooked, in one instance so deep that I had no alternative but to cut the line and hope the fish ejected the hook by itself.

I feel fish welfare should be respected and methods used in catching fish should be given greater thought and consideration when implementing rules and regulations. A total of 33 fish in four sessions should be enough to provide evidence that using indicators aids fish welfare. Takes are seen earlier by the angler, resulting in faster and lighter hooking, which has to cause less harm to the fish. Maybe some anglers know a little more than some fishery managers think they do!

FEBRUARY

Predictable? No chance – not in angling. We can catch fish regularly and frequently on a particular pattern and become complacent in expectation of repeating our success, to the point where in setting up the next day, you expect another good day. As the song lyrics go, "what a difference a day makes" – rings so very true when fishing.

On arrival at Clay Lane 24 short hours after another busy catch and release session, I was greeted with a glorious, bright sunny morning but with a sting in the form of a bitterly cold easterly wind sweeping down the pool. There was no sign of any fish moving, but I knew where they were and what they were taking. At least I thought I did. I set up with the Squirmy Wormy 5ft below the braided loop attached to the fly line and wandered off to the middle of the pool. Cast after cast produced nothing, and I was thinking that the cold wind must have put them down and possibly they had moved to deeper water. I moved steadily down the pool casting all the way until reaching the end, where eventually I managed to bring to the net a very lean and tired-looking rainbow of about 1½ lb.

After several more casts with no response I changed to a corixa, which had produced a few fish recently, but again nothing. Somewhat puzzled at the significant change in attitude from the fish, I went for a brew in the hut and a

serious rethink. On passing the boat I thought perhaps I
should have tried in there!

After a nice brew and some irresistible doughnuts left over
from the previous day by Ray, I was revitalised and warmed
up. Well warmed in fact, as the fire had been left on all night
and it was like walking in to a furnace!

Back to the fishing, and the east wind was still blowing
and the fish were clearly reacting to it by staying put
wherever they were. They certainly were not interested
in my offerings, and I left for home somewhat perplexed a
couple of hours later.

The following day I visited Danebridge fisheries near
Wincle. The wind was still coming from the east, but it was
not as strong and far less cold.

Beginning at the windward end I set up the squirmy again
to try it there. It was on the third cast that my first take was

registered with a sharp pull to the line and a nice rainbow of about 4lb came to the net.

At least the fish here looked as if they would be interested in feeding, as shortly my first was followed by a second. It went quiet for a while, so I went back up to the leeward deeper end of the pool.

A fish soon made its presence there known with a swirl on the surface, which was by now flat calm, and a quick cast

to the ring resulted in another fine rainbow. The fish here seemed to be particularly eager for the squirmy, just as the fish at Clay Lane had been in recent weeks.

I had tweaked the tying of the worm slightly in that I wasn't tying them with thread but sticking them with superglue. I find the thread cuts through the squirmy as it is wound around the hook and breaks off too easily – coating the hook with glue and winding the squirmy around, holding both ends at the required angle until the glue sets, works better and is much quicker too. I also found it gave a much better and more natural imitation of a worm.

Several more quality fish came to the squirmy wormy and I finished my session with eight fish to 5lb. I lost a much larger fish by pulling the hook at the point of netting. A schoolboy error, I know, but these things happen, especially to me.

Session 3 of the month was a visit to the river Dee, accompanied by Millie and Ray, to try for some of the grayling. Millie had since joined the club and Ray was coming as my guest. We decided to meet up at Clay Lane, where Ray was to leave his car and make the journey to Corwen with me. Unfortunately none of us had thought about telling Brian that we would be wanting access at 6:30 that morning, and upon our arrival we were confronted by a locked gate. The three of us gathered at the gate whispering and giggling like school kids on a school outing and not wanting to disturb the teacher. Not one of us had the bottle to knock on Brian's door and get him up to let us in.

I suggested we should simultaneously give a blast of our hooters and flash our headlights to wake the dogs, but we decided that was a bad idea, so we just waited with our engines running in the hope that Brian would eventually make an appearance to see what was going on. It was 15 minutes later when he came to the gate, and with several choice cursory words he let us in and we were swiftly gone.

Our first beat of the day was Chain Pool where Millie set off past the top and Ray began below me. I fished with a heavy Crystal Prince on the point with a single dropper of a Pink Shrimp. It wasn't long before I felt a tug on the line and was rewarded with a nice fish, and Ray had a go of being a photographer, ha ha.

A couple more grayling soon arrived from the same spot and I moved on to allow Millie to have a go. Ray, by this time, had moved down, and he managed a small brownie or salmon parr. He couldn't be sure which species it was and to be fair it is difficult to tell them apart. I thought it was a brownie, as I have caught them in this pool before.

A couple of hours went past in what seemed to be no time at all and the three of us were feeling quite peckish, so we decided to head for Yum Yums, the café bar in town, for a well-earned brew and a sausage and egg bap.

Still dressed in our waders and boots, we sat and enjoyed our beverages whilst looking through past photos and joking

about recent escapades at Clay Lane and so on. It's all part of the enjoyment of the day, but soon it was time for a move and the three of us set off for the Town waters. We parked at the sports ground end and walked to the Run with the intention of fishing all the way down to the Pavilion Pool. I managed to winkle out a grayling from behind the island but kept swiftly moving on, as we had a lot of water to cover. Ray had a fingerling. Millie was still to make contact with a fish, but it didn't matter as we were all learning about the river, and it was the being there that was more important. Well, that's what we keep telling ourselves when we don't catch. But it has to be said that catching is secondary when it comes to the enjoyment of being out in the country, splashing about in a river like immature teenagers and having a laugh.

Walking back to our vehicles after a further couple of fishless hours, we thought we would return to Chain Pool, but there was somebody already occupying the parking spaces, so we moved straight on to Tailors Pool.

This was a lovely stretch of the river and looked in fine fettle, and we thought we were sure to catch here, but alas we didn't and decided to call it a day. The fish weren't playing today, or was it because we were useless at this nymphing lark and couldn't even catch a cold if we stood naked in the river? But what a great day we had. We were already looking forward to our next trip.

The weekend soon arrived and I was back with Kieran. Our meeting was arranged for Danebridge Fisheries and once again it was a rather wet and windy morning. At least the wind was south-westerly and not quite as cold as it had been in recent days. Kieran was keen to try the Squirmy Wormy but preferred to use the Cat's Whisker first and then change later on in the session. With a new leader each and Cat's Whiskers attached, we both set off for the far end, having a few casts on the way as we were the only ones brave enough to endure the elements that were being thrown at us. Neither of us received any interest from fish until we reached the bottom end, and it was Kieran to strike lucky

first. It was a good start to the day. We debated whether or not he should take his first fish, and we decided he should, just in case he failed to catch any more. So this nice rainbow was soon dispatched and put into the bag.

Then it was my turn. A pull on the line close to the nearside bank resulted in my first-ever brownie from this venue.

Kieran stuck with the Cat's for a while longer, but changed to the Squirmy suspended below an orange Blob following a fishless period. I was already using the Squirmy suspended below a bung indicator, which to my surprise attracted three fish before I changed it to a Blob, quickly taking another two fish on the Squirmy before brew time.

It's how when you take a break for a brew the fish often appear to do the same thing, as the second half of the session is rarely as productive as the first. Kieran picked up one more fish soon after returning to the water, as did I, and then another, and Kieran finished the session with his third just before it was time to go.

MARCH

Clay Lane fishery usually continues to fish well in March and Kieran generally gets into the fish using Cat's Whiskers and black buzzers.

Superb early spring weather that year had brought me to try various flies throughout the sessions, but the method that proved unbeatable for me was the Squirmy Wormy. Fished just off the bottom off the drop offs, the fish had been taking this imitative lure/fly like no other, so much so I lost count of the number of fish I had caught. The ban on using any form of indicator hasn't made a jot of difference to my catch rate. It is changes to leader length which make a difference. It's such a simple method if you just want to catch fish.

When I spooned one of Kieran's dispatched fish, I pulled out a pellet that was wrapped in a length of nylon tights and tied to the hook so that it stayed on when casting. With fish taking Buzzers, Cats and Squirmies so readily, it really pains me to understand why people have to resort to cheating. The only people they are fooling are themselves, as they clearly find it difficult to catch fish using legitimate methods.

I joined a syndicate angling association which had the fishing rights to two United Utilities reservoirs on the Cheshire/Derbyshire borders, one of 14 acres and the other 13 acres.

The syndicate has only 30 members, so the waters never get overfished. They are only stocked three times a year, so the catch rates are much lower than your usual small commercial fishery such as Clay Lane. Indeed last year's average per rod was only 2.85.

Looking at a featureless expanse of water was a little daunting at first and deciding where to fish would be very much reliant on my knowledge of watercraft.

When I arrived for my first visit I was greeted by another member who proceeded to fill me in with all sorts of hints and tips that seemed to conflict with my initial thoughts. I listened with some trepidation to what he was going to say next, but his enthusiasm was infectious and I reluctantly followed his advice and tackled up with a Cat's Whisker. He insisted I began at the car park bank, but I hesitated and disagreed. My watercraft suggested I should begin on the side the wind was blowing into, and as my knowledge of this type of water was very limited, I thought the fish would be following along the edges of this leeward bank.

The gentleman urged me to follow him around so he could introduce me to the best fishing points on the reservoir, but I was there to have a few casts and not go for a hike along the banks for the rest of the day, so I politely declined. He pointed out a few best spots, but in fact these places were the only viable casting points on the tree-lined side. I thanked him for his free advice and proceeded toward the open bank on the far side of the car park.

I walked around searching for signs of fish and having the odd cast with the Cat's Whisker on the way, until I finally arrived at the area I had in mind. I hadn't seen any signs of fish all the way round and began to wonder if my fellow member could have been right in saying I should begin on the windward side.

I began casting into the wind, surprisingly obtaining good distance with the advantage of the high banking, and took my first fish after five or six casts. An extremely spirited fight ensued and the fish lunged several times into the depths of the reservoir's clear water, before a 2lb-plus rainbow eventually came to the net.

After several more unproductive casts with the Cat's, I changed tactic to the Squirmy, putting on a bung and tying a Wormy 6ft below. The bung bobbed up and down in the ripple on the surface, which was sure to be making the worm move tantalisingly, and it wasn't long before another fish pulled the line. They certainly do fight well here, and after a good scrap another fine rainbow of similar size to the first came to the net. Hard as it fought coming to the net, it zoomed back to freedom with just as much fight and energy still left in it.

Three more quality rainbows soon followed before it was time for me to leave, quite happy with my first visit to a water I had never seen before.

A second visit to Clay Lane with Kieran was pretty much a repeat performance of the previous session, and the weather was very similar too, with clear skies and a light breeze from the south west. Perfect conditions for this venue, as it brings on a midge hatch that lasts for several hours, though this is mainly in the mornings.

Kieran was pleased with his take-home bag of two fish, both caught on buzzer, although for different reasons he lost five others whilst playing them.

So that was March over and done with. It was so nice to have some warm sunshine on our backs as I looked forward now to an even better April.

APRIL

The month began with another visit to Disley reservoirs and an almost repeat performance of my first. I used a Squirmy set 6ft below a bung fishing over on the cabin side of the top reservoir. I couldn't see any fish rising or up in the water anywhere across the reservoir. Once again the wind was coming from the south-west, much as it had been for the past week, and I thought this bank was the most likely to hold a few fish. My assumption was correct, and it wasn't long before the bung disappeared for the first time and a fish was on.

Not a huge fish by any means, but as these reservoir stockies do, it put up a long and hard fight, lunging and leaping and trying to throw the fly. Another four fish followed to the same tactic until I was getting bored with monotonous casting and decided to finish my session after three hours.

A couple more sessions with Kieran at Clay Lane Mobberley were something of a repeat performance of the previous visits, with Kieran catching on Squirmy and Buzzers and taking home two fish.

Entomology seemed to be catching on at the fishery, since as I started spooning Kieran's dispatched fish other anglers followed suit, or went pond dipping if they didn't want to dispatch fish. Matching the hatch and imitating natural aquatic insects is an essential part of fly-fishing and helps the angler to make informed decisions on fly choices. For example, if we find chironomid larvae and pupa in a fish's stomach then the sensible fly to use is a buzzer to match the colour and size of the natural. However, this sounds all too obvious when watercourses sustain different aquatic life in different areas.

When I spooned a fish at the top end of the pool the stomach contents were full of daphnia, with only a couple of chironomid larvae (as in the picture below).

The second fish spooned was from the middle section of the pool, within minutes of the first, and my findings were completely different. This fish's stomach contents consisted of only caddis fly larva cases, with one larva clearly visible still in its case (commonly known to anglers as the Peeping Caddis).

So, decisions, decisions... both fish were caught on Squirmy!

My next session was a day to myself to try out a couple of different flies I had tied. I don't profess to be the greatest fly tier ever, but I believe that if a fly resembles something like a natural, then the fish will have a go at it. Professionally-tied flies look beautiful, but do they catch any more fish? I believe it is more about how the flies are fished than what they look like. If your fly resembles the size and shape of a natural and is made to behave like a natural, then you're on to a winner.

An Emerger style surface fly   A battered Copper Pheasant
Tail Nymph

Fished on different types of leaders, lines and lengths, these flies certainly fooled the fish this month and as a final bonus I took my first 3lb plus golden orfe of the year. I think I can say I April-fooled 'em!

MAY

So there I was thinking not much was going to happen this month having not booked my usual week to Scotland, so with only a couple of sessions booked with Kieran at Mobberley and a couple of visits to Disley Reservoirs, I decided to have a week off work and arrange some local river fishing for brown trout. To be fair the fishing had been great on the still waters, with me notching up 31 fish in my two visits to Disley despite water levels being low.

The Squirmy was still working well at Mobberley and taking the majority of fish, but I was beginning to get bored with that method in the clear waters.

To stimulate my brain with something that needed more concentration, I decided to stalk and tease out fish with the copper Pheasant Tail Nymph. The fish seem to go mad for it and I was getting follows nearly every cast. I had not quite perfected the skill of hooking up on every follow, but I was getting there with about an 80% success rate. Much more exciting than just chucking out and waiting for fish to take the bait so to speak. Fly-fishing is so engrossing.

My week off from work arrived and Millie was at my door at 7:30 on the Monday morning in anticipation of the unexpected. He hadn't been to the River Dove before and hadn't done any research on the beat either. Fancy him thinking he was going to use his Tenkara "stick". Tut tut.

I met the river keeper at the Charles Cotton Hotel in Hartington, and he confirmed that the river was low and with the bright conditions forecast for the day it would be a challenging time for us intrepid piscators hoping to follow in the footsteps of Izaac Walton.

Millie wasn't fussed about old stories about the venue, he just wanted to get fishing and didn't even want a photo taken of him on the steps of angling history. I even brought with me my 1889 edition of *The Compleat Angler* so I could recite a few lines to him about studying to be quiet and that angling was the contemplative sport of gentlemen and scholars, but he didn't want to know. Oh well, I tried my best.

We tackled up over a brew, and I insisted that Millie should use conventional upstream dry fly and nymph tactics in order to preserve some dignity in the skills of angling, which to be honest is not high on the agenda at stocked stillwater venues.

Setting off together, we began in the temple grounds and on the second cast I hooked into a small brownie that jumped from the water instantaneously and threw the hook. My confidence was boosted. Millie wandered off downstream, while I decided to make my way upstream toward the beat's upper limit.

Now I'm 59 years of age and weigh a little over 15 stone, so creeping around on all fours becomes ponderous, as I soon experienced when my steadying hand slipped down a hole in the ground and my overweight torso rocketed off down the bank, leaving me spread-eagled in a patch of early-season stinging nettles. Cursing aloud, I pulled myself up, wincing at the tingling sensation to my inner left arm whilst probably spooking every fish within 20 yards of my uncontrolled approach.

Moving on upstream I noticed several small brownies darting to and fro in all directions as they saw me in the clearer, shallower water. Finally I came to a deep corner where I decided to crouch down behind the vegetation to do a bit of speculating, as no fish were visible. I was using a small copper PTN and cast toward the near bank. As it hit the surface an almighty swirl engulfed the nymph and a good fish was on. Alas it wasn't a resident wild brownie but an out of season grayling of around 2lb.

A welcome alternative to my sought-after quarry.

On a small river like this I would normally rest a swim after catching a fish, but as this was a grayling I thought where there's one there are normally two, and although they were out of season I cheekily cast again. After a couple a blank casts another grayling took my nymph. I was sure there would be more, but it was the wild brown trout I was after, so I left them alone.

The sun was getting higher in the sky and the temperature was rising, which was more than the fish were doing. There was no sign of any trout except the little darters. I managed to pick one of them off before getting my only proper wild brownie of the day on a small Grey Wulff.

A couple more grayling fell to the nymph later in the afternoon, but disappointingly there was no hatch of any kind to encourage fish to rise throughout the day. Millie found three browns lower down the beat, probably because of the tree cover there, and I was in an open field. I'm sure the fish were there but they stayed put under the weed or hard into the banks. It was a good day out though, and it was nice to return to the hallowed ground.

An early rise for me the next morning and I was off to Ilkley in Yorkshire. My wife and I had visited the town a couple of weeks before and I purchased an Ilkley Angling Club day ticket in advance to fish the river Wharfe and booked into the Riverside Hotel for a night so I could fish the Bolton Abbey stretch the following day. When I arrived at the river at 8 am the sun was already warming up the air and drying off the overnight dew on the grass. The water level was well down as expected, there having been no significant rainfall for several weeks, or months even.

In truth I wasn't expecting a day of constant catching with the conditions against me and the low cost of the day ticket speaks for itself, indicating that it is not a stocked fishery. But I was there and it's the exploring of a new river that is the attraction for me.

Fully kitted up with waders, I ventured out to the middle of the river armed with my #3 rod. The water was barely coming up to my knees at the access point, but there was a deeper glide on the far bank where I thought I could find a fish or two. I began with a small copper PTN under a Klinkhamer, Klink and Dink as some people call it. It was after 3 runs through that my Klink disappeared and I struck into my first fish on the Dink. Hoping it was going to be a wild brownie I played it carefully as it put up a decent fight in the current, when it became obvious it was a grayling. Again, out of season maybe but still very welcome none the less.

Wandering upstream to the suspension footbridge, I disturbed several shoals of fry, tens of thousands of this year's naturally-reared generation. Although most will succumb to predation in one way or another, it was good to see a healthy river.

As I approached one end of the bridge, a welcome sight was to behold at the other. The local ice cream van had parked up for a while and I thought it would be rude to ignore his refreshing delights, so a 99 cone was ordered. It was massive and it took a while to devour as I sat on a rock beside the river in gorgeous sunshine listening to the riffling of the water and the birds in the trees. Could things get any better than this?

Well they did! As I waded back downstream, the mayfly were beginning to hatch. They would appear from nowhere on the water surface and fly off towards the trees. I visually followed one as it flew under the tree canopy and bounced on the water surface. Unfortunately, it rested for too long and a trout came up and woofed it down. I had mixed emotions at that point; sad for the mayfly for its life to end so suddenly after hatching, before having the chance to mate, and happiness that I had spotted a feeding trout.

Time for a change of tactic for me, and I tied on a large green Drake to "match the hatch". My first cast was a little short of where the fish rose, so I let it drift past and recast again right under the tree canopy and let it ride with the current, and sure enough the fish rose again and took it. My first trout of the day was on. Proper angling that, I thought to myself!

On a high, I packed up for the afternoon to check in to the hotel and nip up to Bolton Abbey to have a look around. Unfortunately I couldn't purchase a day ticket in advance, so I went back for a rest until the evening, when I thought there may be a serious mayfly hatch happening down by the bridge. But there wasn't. To my surprise hardly anything at all was coming off, so I put on the Klinkhamer and nymph again and managed a couple more small grayling. I still had time to persevere for another trout, but my empty belly was grumbling and telling me it needed food, so I gave in and went back to the hotel, where I was well fed and watered.

The next morning, after a full English breakfast, I returned to Bolton Abbey to purchase my day ticket and set off to the section I wanted to fish. It was nice easy access and comfortable wading for me today.

The main object of my day was to use North Country Spiders, which would be another first for me. I have been watching some videos of Oliver Edwards fishing this method and thought it would be good to have a go. They are a very sparsely-dressed wet fly and easy to tie, so that's right up my street. However on arrival there were no fish showing themselves, so the favourable 'klink and dink' method was chosen to begin with.

Whilst I was sitting on the grass tackling up, a fish did actually show itself over in the darker, tree-covered water. Gingerly, I crept to the water's edge and cast a little upstream of where I saw the rise, and as the Klink reached this point, it went under and I struck into my first fish of the day on my first cast. It was only a little brown, so it went back straight away without having to go through the indignity of having its photo taken.

This stretch of the river is lightly stocked each month through the season in order to give the angler a better chance of a higher catch return.

Another brown and a nice grayling followed quickly as I wandered upstream, casting into any likely area that could hold a fish or two. I even tried the much shallower riffles as the weather was more overcast than the previous day, successfully plucking out another grayling. I decided to keep on the move quite a lot, as I wanted to explore as much of this beat as I could in the time given. I wanted to be back home early evening.

I reached the point of the Cavendish Café, ideally located beside the river by early afternoon. After experiencing a blank spell as the sky cleared and the sun got brighter in the sky, other anglers on the beat, as well as myself, were also struggling. I speculated that a fish could be in near to the bank as I cast out right in front of me, and not surprisingly another grayling took the copper PTN.

The browns were conspicuous by their absence as I

returned downstream. At about three o'clock I reached a deeper, slower section of the river where rises were abundant from several fish throughout the entire 60-yard run. Spider time, I thought, and changed my set-up to a black on the point, a Partridge and Orange on second dropper and a Snipe and Purple on the top dropper.

Waiting for a rise within easy casting distance, as the wind was now gusting downstream, I cast out and waited for a pull. I received my first indication of a fish, but failing to connect. This happened a couple of times until I realised that if I waited for a line pull after a rise I was too late, so I began striking at the rise rather than anything else and hey presto, I was straight into a fish.

My first North Country Spider caught a brown trout, which took the Partridge and Orange. By now there were rises constantly appearing and a definite hatch going on, so I stayed put and had another three from the same spot without moving at all. It went quiet after a while, so eventually I moved a little further down the pool, where I began catching more fish of similar size. I spent a couple of hours moving up and down this pool, catching browns quite regularly, all on the Partridge and Orange. I ended up with 11 browns and three grayling before I decided to call it a day. To be honest I could have stayed catching for much longer, but again my hunger was telling me otherwise, so I left, quite contented with my efforts.

I couldn't resist a quick visit to Mobberley the next day, just to practise the sink and draw with a copper PTN, catching five rainbows and two baby golden orfe within a couple of hours before having a brew and then off home. Well it has to be done, doesn't it!

Friday morning I got my wife up early and said that if she would come to Disley Reservoir with me for a couple of hours I would buy her breakfast at Wetherspoons afterwards. How could she refuse an offer like that? So off we went, arriving

at 7:30, and I began near the car park without seeing any fish in the near vicinity.

The water level was even lower than before, so a move down amongst the trees was called for. It was here I found several fish, and five came to the net quite quickly. By 9 am the belly alarm was going off, so we hot-footed to Wetherspoons for a full English. Sorted!

What was I using? A Squirmy of course! And Bev enjoyed the trip as well. She would never admit to it, but she did!

So here we were at the end of May and it really had flown past, with only a handful of mayfly spotted on the Wharfe. In all the years I had been fishing I had never witnessed one of nature's greatest aquatic spectacles, a full-on mayfly hatch, and it looked like I was going to have to wait a bit longer.

An early morning drive down south on the Monday morning gave me ample time to visit another stillwater that I had never been to before – Meon Springs, near Petersfield. I had seen on their website they did a catch-and-release ticket on two of their pools, a rarity in the south of England. It's a fabulous setup, and if you wanted to take fish you don't have to nominate your bag limit before commencing fishing, unlike most. You just sign in, start fishing and pay at the end. If you decide to take a single fish, two or even three, then you just pay for them when you leave. Excellent!

It was an overcast, damp morning with little wind when I arrived, and on reaching the bottom pool there were no fish showing themselves in the gin-clear water.
The surface was dead flat and the slightest sign of disturbance from a fly line landing on it would send ripples the entire length and spook any fish within 20 yards. A long leader was

necessary today. Looking more closely into the clear depths, I saw a few fish wallowing about at around the 4ft level, but they were not showing any indications of feeding. I would have to induce a take with a nymph. My trusty old copper PTN was tied to an 18ft long leader attached to my #5 rod and floating line.

I persevered for about an hour before getting my first induced take and a small rainbow graced my landing net. It was only about 1¼lb, but at least I wasn't going to blank today.

Staying with the same method, I continued to walk around the bottom pool. I saw a few more fish moving about and being a whole lot more active, and it wasn't too long before I hit into my first brown trout at Meon Springs. Again, not a huge fish, but this did seem to be the stamp of fish that are stocked into these catch and release pools.

As I ventured up to the second pool, which is much smaller than the first, the density of fish seemed to be greater. There was a group of fish feeding under the reflection of the tree to the right, so creeping round I cast my nymph and received some interest, but no takes. These fish seemed spookier than the others on the bottom pool, probably because a couple of anglers had already been targeting them earlier without success. They were sipping at the surface and appeared to be taking small emerging midges. I took off a few feet of my leader, tied on a lower diameter tippet and put a tiny size

18 CDC Emerger on, and first cast I hooked but lost a nice brown. The commotion put the fish off for a few minutes, but they soon returned and normal service was resumed.

Another brown took my fly and this time it didn't get away until I released it.

Switching to a Klinkhamer, I picked off another two fish and ended my first visit to this venue with three browns and two rainbows. I decided I would definitely return here when I got back down to Sussex/Hampshire in the near future. The venue has all the amenities an angler needs – tackle shop, café, toilets etc.

The main reason for my visit down south had arrived and I was due to meet the Fishing TV crew at 9 am at Bullington for a day's filming of CHALK on the River Dever, a carrier of the Upper River Test. CHALK is a film about the past present and future of the chalkstreams of England, and a thoughtful examination of why the chalkstreams of England are probably the most important rivers in the history and development of fly fishing. The film covers everything from the geology that created the rivers and their abundant plant and animal life - including the legendary mayfly hatch - to the characters past, present and future who make these rivers unique. The film celebrates the rivers while also drawing attention to the threats and challenges facing these fragile environments

I was to fish with a gentleman and his wife from Surrey, whom I had never met before.

After a coffee and a chat about the format for the day, we set off. This was going to be another new experience for me as I had only fished a chalk stream once before, and that was the River Kennet at Kintbury in Berkshire the previous summer.

I started off with a 7ft 6in #3 rod, but found this to be too short to reach over the nearside vegetation, so it would not give me enough control for nymphing. I put on a dry fly, even though few fish, if any were rising. I persevered with this method of upstream casting until it was time to head back to the cabin without a fish for the mid-morning brew. I was feeling a bit anxious about not catching anything with the film crew hovering around me, but I was then secretly relieved to hear the others hadn't caught either. I switched to my 9ft #5, scaled down the tippet size and began using a small beaded Pheasant Tail Nymph for the rest of the day.

This proved to be a wise decision. I was far too busy catching fish to bother taking any photographs, leaving that job to the skills of the crew. I remained with the PTN until early evening, when I was asked to change to the Mayfly. I cast at and over fish for a couple of hours with only one take, which I missed through impaired vision – I was looking the other way, towards the cameras. DOH! Just for the record though, I caught 25 browns, five grayling and a minnow on the PTN. The others had two browns between them on the mayfly. Oops!

JUNE

The month began where May left off, warm and sunny with only a day's worth of steady rain giving a small rise to the rivers for a short period, only for them to fall back to the lower summer levels within 24 hours.

I hadn't booked a trip to Scotland that year because of other events in my calendar, and I was quite pleased I hadn't. Because of the low river levels the salmon weren't entering the system and the resident fish were having none of it, so catch returns were lower than average. If I had gone I probably would have blanked again anyway and wished that I hadn't bothered, so I was happy to stay local for the month and try some alternative flies at Clay Lane, Mobberley.

Most fly fishers have an uncontrollable obsession to possess more flies than they can ever use, whether commercially tied or self-tied. It's an addiction to have all sizes, colours and patterns in their fly boxes, and I'm no exception. We do this even though we all go back to the same proven patterns that we know work and have been successful many times over – we must have something different at hand, just in case. Most flies stay in the box and never get a day out, so I was determined that my sessions at Clay Lane this month would be the time to try something new. Subconsciously I knew that after a couple of hours into fishing a four-hour session I would change back to a tried and tested fly if I hadn't caught by then.

It wasn't difficult to select unused flies from my boxes as I have dozens of them, but I would choose wisely according to the conditions, except that being summer I wasn't going to bother with lures. At this time of year there is an abundance of natural fly life from nymphs, buzzers and dries that inhabit this water so, I was thinking there would be little point in whizzing a Humungous or a Cat's Whisker past the fish. In any case my preferred method is sight fishing or stalking, rather than chucking and chancing.

Coincidentally my workplace at that time was just around the corner from Clay Lane, so Paul and I pinched a couple of hours out of our day to have quick thrash. Paul hadn't fly fished for about three years, so he was a bit rusty with his casting. He asked me to demonstrate a few short casts before he began, just to refresh him. I chose the narrowest part of the pool, where I knew a few fish resided, and third cast I latched on to a fish using a buzzer under a Stimulator dry fly. I set Paul up with a similar outfit but using a Klinkhamer in place of the Stimulator, and it wasn't long before he was into his first fish.

After a few casts around the pool, whilst giving that area a rest, we soon returned, and each quickly hooked and

landed our second fish of the session, concluding a pleasant time away from work.

Getting back to my plans of trying out unused flies, I began another session by sinking and drawing nymphs on a short line. I was getting some interest but no takes on various patterns of Diawl Bach. Changing back to a tried and tested Flashback PTN proved successful, and a nice rainbow put up a sprightly fight on my #5 Streamflex rod.

I wondered why they ignored the Diawl Bach and nailed the PTN when they were fished the same way and to all intense and purposes looked very similar. Well, to me anyway.

A few of the golden orfe were cruising around near the surface, so I switched leaders and put on a Shuttlecock. I cast to a single fish on its own and instantly it took the fly. Orfe don't put up much of a fight, but they are gorgeous fish to look at. Although I hadn't used this particular pattern of fly on this water before, I have caught elsewhere on similar, but with a different coloured thorax.

For my next few sessions the weather had turned. It was very unsettled on each occasion and the water colour had changed dramatically with the rain. I stuck to my guns in using untried flies without success and notched up a couple of blanks in succession. Was it me, or could I blame the changing conditions? But then, talking of changing conditions, flaming

June took hold. Record temperatures hit the country and our stillwaters warmed up quickly. The aerators were put on to increase the oxygen levels, which increased the turbidity even more, but on my penultimate visit of the month to Clay Lane, unknown to me, it had been restocked. There seemed to be few fish showing up and down the pool except at the house end, where I stayed for a couple of hours and had 12 fish in quick succession using buzzers under a Stimulator. I frequently changed the buzzer to different patterns and sizes and it seemed the smaller size in green and black did the trick.

My final session of the month was the following day. I blanked again, bringing an end to a not-so-successful June. Three blanks in a month that should otherwise be quite productive brought me to the conclusion that I should stick with fly patterns that I know and trust if I wanted to catch fish regularly. But what should I do with those flies that were unsuccessful and just sat in the box for all time – should I discard them or keep them just in case?

I think I really know the answer to that question!

JULY

In midsummer I always get excited about using the dry fly. Okay, we can use them all year round, but July is the month when I mostly concentrate on surface tactics. With an abundance of naturals in and on the water, it can sometimes become mind-boggling when choosing an artificial pattern to use. So many choices in the fly box makes it even harder. There is always a go-to fly that I know works at Clay Lane, but sometimes I want a change, whether the fish are wanting one or not. Presenting something different never fails to give me that additional buzz when a fish rises and takes that alternative bit of fluff that to my eyes resembles nothing like a natural.

My first session of the month was at Danebridge Fisheries near Macclesfield. Arriving mid-morning, I was surprised to find I was the only one there. The conditions were pretty much perfect for dry fly-fishing, broken cloud with little breeze producing a slight ripple on the water and the air temperature was nice and cool.

Knowing that there was a possibility of hooking up with a large fish, I tackled up on my Sage #7 rod. A 5.5lb tapered leader and a 5lb tippet would be sufficient to play the fish hard enough without fear of a break-off. Several fish were rising in all areas of the lake, so it didn't need much thought on where to begin. The fish were taking black gnats, which were swarming over the surface, and again it wasn't a difficult decision on what fly I was going to tie on my tippet.

It wasn't long before I got into the action and a few nice plump rainbows were brought to the net. The first was all of 4lb. I changed my fly on several occasions to see if the fish were fixated on the gnat and would take anything else. For the next hour or so the takes did slow down. The fish were happy to investigate many patterns that I tried, but weren't as confident in taking them as the gnat. I managed to land five and release (lose) a couple at distance in the following hour or so.

About midday the gnats simply disappeared and the fish stopped rising altogether; they disappeared down into the depths, never to be seen again. Not by me that day, anyway. I suppose I could have tried a buzzer or nymph deeper down, but I couldn't be bothered to change my leader, so that was that and I finished my session quite satisfied.

Which is more than I could say for the following session at the weekend, a return visit with Millie. I arrived at Danebridge a little after 10 am following a meeting with clients in Macclesfield to find Millie casting away to his heart's content. He commented "Where the heck have you been?" and "What time do you call this?" That's actually putting it politely. Millie did in fact add a few other expletives to his "good morning Mike" welcome!

The day was bright, warm and very still with a few fish rising. By the time I had set up, Millie was landing his first fish, which would also be his last fish of the day. I didn't do any better, as I only managed the one fish on a Klinkhamer. The fish did the same disappearing trick as the previous visit, only much earlier in the day, probably because of the bright sunshine. There's always an excuse. I persevered with the dry in the hope of an occasional rise, but saw only a couple of fish come up and nose the fly, showing no more interest than that. Again, I'm sure that had I tried the buzzer or nymph I might well have had a few more fish, but it's July and I'm fishing the dry – end of!

A session after work at Clay Lane beckoned, as it had been a while since my last visit. Well, seven days is quite a while this time of year. The water was looking decidedly odd. The colour was a greyish blue and looked almost stagnant, with a translucent film on the surface. Even more noticeable was that there was no algae blanket weed anywhere to be seen. There had been plenty only a week or so before. Had something been put in, mysteriously killing off the weed, I wondered?

There were no trout showing and no sign of the ever-present golden orfe either. How strange! The catch return book was showing blanks from several anglers, which was also unusual. But for now I was here, and here I was going to stay, for a while anyway. In my two-hour session I managed to pluck out two trout and a young orfe on my Flashback PTN. There was nothing rising and a dry fly would have been a complete waste of effort.

The following couple of sessions would be almost repeat performances, with only one and two fish respectively on the PTN, and others too were struggling on the fishery. My dry fly only plan for the month was faltering very quickly.

The weather was faltering as well, with the middle of the month bringing much-needed rain to our depleted waterways. The syndicate water at Disley was dropping significantly as United Utilities drew off drinking water for the East Manchester region. One of the syndicate membership stipulations is that every member must attend a working party at least once a year. By a complete coincidence, I planned to attend a working party and stocking of the reservoir on a very rare day it was lumping down with rain and the work party was cancelled, so a couple of hours' fishing could be done prior to the new stocking.

The water level was probably more than 15ft below capacity, reducing the water volume considerably. Several fish were rising to emergers, and knowing there was an abundance of caddis on the water I chose a sedge pattern and was soon landing my first fish and then my second. Five fish seemed to be an appropriate number to stop before meeting up with the other members for the stocking. I was absolutely soaked when I reached the cabin and was greeted with laughter by the others when I arrived.

The re-stocking began with 375 fighting-fit rainbows to 3lb going in. Carrying the bins of fish by human chain, the fish were all safely introduced to their new home, and I resumed where I had left off, still soaking wet, for another hour, picking off another two rainbows from the surface. It was getting a little silly standing there in the pouring rain just catching fish for the sake of it, so I decided enough was enough and set off home to dry out my wet weather gear for the weekend.

Thinking that Clay Lane might have improved after the rain, I set off at the weekend for another short session. Nothing much had changed except the colour of the water, which was now a murky brown. I spotted a few fish about 2ft down, so I gave it a go with a Shipman's Buzzer, in the full knowledge that I had only ever caught one fish on this fly in all my years fishing this venue. It just seemed a good idea at the time. An unsurprisingly fruitless idea as it turned out, as nothing was remotely interested and I soon lost interest too.

Changing my Shipman's to a Flashback PTN, I moved to the aerator swim and on the second cast I had a small rainbow. Millie had arrived, and by some fluke he had taken a couple of fish on a buzzer suspended under a Klinkhamer. That was what he told me he was using, but I wasn't so sure. He then walked up to me and chucked some floating trout pellets into my zone. A few fish took advantage of these free offerings, woofing them down, and I thought this was my cue to leave, finishing the month on a disappointing wet low.

AUGUST

I have had the pleasure of being able to fish in many stunning locations up and down the UK, in fast-flowing rivers and tranquil stillwaters, but no other watercourse holds more visible aquatic life to the angler than the chalkstream. They all look similar, and yet they all seem different. I've been lucky enough to fish three of the country's greatest chalkstreams within 12 months, the Kennet at Kintbury, the Test at Stockbridge, Hampshire and most recently the lesser known Mulberry Whin on Driffield Beck, Yorkshire.

Driffield Beck is a highly-valued chalkstream in the eastern Wolds, the most northerly point on earth where alkaline aquifer-fed rivers exist. It rises as a spring at Elmswell in the foothills of the Yorkshire Wolds and flows for a little over 10 miles until it joins the River Hull 19 miles from the sea.

Bev and I arrived at the cabin at 9 am on the most perfect day (well, it was my birthday). Actually it can never be perfect for us anglers, as there is always something not quite right for fishing. The wind was gusting downstream, which would make casting upstream a little difficult with the light lines and rods best suited for these clear waters. A few light clouds began to form, giving us welcome breaks from the strong sunshine just at the right time.

I set up with two rods, a 4lb tapered leader with a 3.3lb tippet for nymphing on a 9ft #5 Streamflex and 3.3lb tapered

leader with a 3.1lb tippet for dry fly on a 7'6" #3 Streamflex. A short walk across a field led us to the river, where we were greeted by a family of swans who seemed quite pleased to see us, probably thinking an alternative breakfast had just arrived. Sadly not though.

The access point is in the middle of the beat and having no prior knowledge or advice, I decided to go downstream and work my way back up. That was going to be the plan anyway. As I quietly walked or crept down behind the bankside vegetation, there was too much of an urge not to have a few casts at the fish I could see. Fishing with a tiny tungsten beaded Pheasant Tail Nymph, I made my first cast to a group of fish in the middle of a gravel run beside some ranunculus. With no indicator and a single fly, the skill lies with the angler to watch the fish's movement, judging where the nymph is and striking when a fish moves, but only when you think the nymph has been taken.

On my third cast I struck into a little wild rainbow. I chose to release this fish because I was in a state of confusion about the fishery rules. When I had read the rules prior to fishing I found them to be somewhat ambiguous. They stated at the cabin that all rainbows must be killed, yet the website stated that it was catch and release only, and if that wasn't confusing enough the rules on another site said that two fish may be taken over 11 inches. Until I could clarify the rules with Will the river keeper, all my fish were going to be returned.

Moving on downstream the fish were in abundance, but very spooky. One bad cast in this wind with the line falling too heavily on the surface and they would be gone. This chalkstream fishing isn't as easy as would first appear to a non-angler (the wife) as she quietly smirked, thinking to herself that it must be easy to drop a fly on all those fish. Embarrassingly though, I hooked the far bank or the line would blow back on me into an overhanging tree on more than one occasion.

In spite of a few miscasts, it was not before long I was into my first brown, and it was a good size, just under 3lb. What a cracking start to the day! A couple of smaller brownies came to the net before it was time to head back to the cabin for a mid-morning brew.

Suitably refreshed and with leaders and tippets tweaked, we ventured off upstream, where the river took on a very different appearance, giving way to deeper pools, more weed and a siltier bottom. There were also noticeably fewer fish visible to stalk and target. Larger fish could well have been in residence hiding in the depths under strands of weed, but as I only had the one day available to me I wasn't going to waste time speculating.

Another three fish were landed before I reached the end of the beat and Will, the river keeper, showed up. I was fully satisfied with my catch thus far. He clarified the rules, confirming that pretty much any fly-fishing method was permissible. An interesting conversation about the contradictory rules ensued as we made our way back to the cabin for lunch, where fresh sandwiches, cakes and doughnuts were beckoning.

Although easier methods were now available to me, such as downstream casting and multiple use of flies and streamers, I kept to the more traditional upstream casting of single nymph and dry flies. I prefer to test my angling skills in accurate casting rather than let the fish jump on the hook as the fly falls into their mouths as it does with a downstream method, or chucking and chancing with a streamer. My casting accuracy did improve as the day progressed, and even the wife was quite impressed at the end.

Working my way back downstream after lunch, a few more browns were brought to the net. Then I noticed a couple of large grayling on the edge of a nearside weed bed. I needed to cast over the weed without the line hitching up on it, so using an indicator above the PTN was my only option, apart from wading up the river from downstream and risk spooking other fish. So I cast over the weed, allowing the nymph to settle above and in front of the fish. The indicator buried as it floated over the nose of a fish and I struck into my first grayling of the day. There followed a sprightly tussle to keep the fish from diving deep into the thicket of weed and throwing the hook, and Bev thought it quite amusing as I slid into the water to retrieve the fish amongst the mass of weed with my landing net.

A fin perfect 2½ lb grayling was safely landed and quietly obliged for a photo shoot. A fitting moment to end the most perfect day with 18 brown trout, two rainbows and one grayling. Magical!

August had got off to a great start with the visit to Mulberry Whin, but it quickly went downhill from there on, as far as catching fish was concerned anyway. Stillwaters, especially

Clay Lane at Mobberley, never fish as well in August, due to high water temperatures and low oxygen levels. These conditions make the fish lethargic and they will mostly loiter around the deeper and cooler water. They seemingly wait to feed in the cooler evening for the final fly hatch of the day just before dark, picking off any nymphs and emergers as and when the urge takes them.

In all the years I have fished Clay Lane, I have never before fished an evening session until dusk. However, Kieran was available for a couple of midweek evening sessions, so I picked him up after work and we headed off to Mobberley. It was a typical bright, warm August afternoon, barely conjuring up a breath of air to form a ripple on the water surface. As we drove up to the cabin we came upon a sparrowhawk which was standing in defiance over its afternoon meal of a freshly-caught pigeon. It gave us a look of contempt as we passed. There was a standoff for several minutes as we watched it tuck in to the fresh meat. Who was going to move first? As I edged closer, it became obvious that this raptor was not for turning. We had eye to eye contact as I moved over to the right, passing it close by, while Kieran was hanging out of the window commenting on its lack of fear and determination not to leave its kill. After a while it finished its meal and flew

off into the trees.

Some of the wonders of nature we anglers see when fishing never ceases to thrill. It's an added incentive for us to do what we do, and it puts catching fish into a close second place. Who cares about catching fish on a gorgeous summer's evening when you can just sit quietly and watch the wildlife, actually being amongst it?

The coots and moorhens scurry about the water fighting territorial battles with their neighbours. Birds sing in the hedgerows and trees. Butterflies, damsels and dragonflies flutter past as they seek a mate. Little grebes dive and pop up several metres away from where they went down, searching for food. A little fieldmouse makes a swim for it across a corner of the pool, I can't think why. And then fish begin to rise, but not for hatched adult flies. They are taking emergers just below the surface. I am unable to determine what they are, until I notice a group of flies dancing amongst the tips of the marginal vegetation. Have you ever tried to catch flies in the hand as they fly past? It's like the film clip in Karate Kid of catching a fly with the tips of a pair of chopsticks. Eventually I caught one, but unfortunately I crushed it beyond all recognition in my sweaty palm. It was some time before I managed to identify them as brown silverhorn, a small variety of caddis or sedge. I had never seen these flies at any other time of day on this water before. The fish became fixated on them, but only for a short time. As quickly as they came on the feed they stopped again and disappeared back into the depths. Kieran and I tried all kinds of emergers, CDC and buzzer patterns without as much of a sniff. I was going to have to tie some flies to match these little fellows for our next evening session.

That session soon arrived and I had managed to tie a few CDC emergers to hopefully match the forth coming evenings hatch. It was a bit of a rerun of our first evening session, but the skies were a little more moody, so much so there was a storm brewing in the distance.

You could almost set your clocks by the repeat performance of nature's events as the fish began to rise one hour before dusk. A switch to my newly-tied emergers produced what seemed a miracle as the fish took to them as never before. One after another came to the fly, and I had four hook-ups in quick succession, missing I don't know how many. Unfortunately Kieran didn't succeed in achieving a hook up, but he enjoyed the fact that fish were showing interest on an otherwise fruitless evening.

As the storm grew closer, there seemed to be an eerily silence about the place as the birds stopped singing and the coots, moorhens and little grebes roosted for the night. Even the silverhorn display ceased and it appeared nature was put on hold for the time being as it was time for us to leave.

These high water temperatures of August are not as detrimental to some species of fish as they are to the trout. The golden orfe seem to flourish in these conditions and love to spawn. Every year they produce a shoal of several thousand fry, and I find it fun to catch a few on a small buzzer. It passes a few minutes when the trout aren't playing the game. Size isn't everything, is it!

It's all about being there with nature and witnessing the natural wonders of our countryside, like the unmistaken silent blue flash of the kingfisher flying just above the waterline, apparently faster than the speed of sound.

There's the unmistakable mewing cry of a buzzard circling high above as it soars on a thermal updraft. There's the surprise of seeing a newt almost at my feet ascending for a breath of air before descending back to the murky depths of its home. Or the magical appearance of a pond olive lifting from the water surface while a trout leaps clear to engulf another hatching relative. There is so much more on offer to the angler than catching fish.

SEPTEMBER

This month started off with a couple of sessions with Kieran at Mobberley, which resulted in a disappointing blank on the first and a solitary fish on the second. A lack of dissolved oxygen in the not-so-cool water was making the fish as lethargic as they were back in August. They were just wallowing around in the unrelenting bright conditions. The aerators at both ends of the pool were continuously working flat out to pump oxygen back into the water.

It was very much the same on the Disley syndicate water, which I have never seen so low. Early morning sessions were producing a handful of fish, but leaving it later in the day was a pointless exercise.

On another visit to Mobberley I was surprised to learn that it had been restocked. There were plenty of fish in there already, although they were difficult to catch, which was quite evident by the catch return book, featuring more blanks than scores.

Scaling down to a #3 rod and 0.13 tippet, the fish were coming to my flashback Pheasant Tail Nymph. The quality of fish though was poor and quite an embarrassment. They were quite possibly some of the poorest quality stocked fish I have ever seen. However, scaling down did the trick and several fish were landed in my two-hour session.

It was too much of a temptation not to make one more visit to Mobberley before my week in North Wales, fishing the River Dee. The catch return book was again showing a number of blanks and the anglers that had caught only caught one or two. I couldn't understand it, as there were so many fish cruising about near the surface that I felt they must be catchable. I set up a FPTN on 0.13 and a #3 rod and away I went, getting a fish first cast. This repeated itself time after time during the day whilst others were struggling to catch. This time the majority of the fish were of slightly better quality than my previous session.

Fifteen rainbows came to this method during the session and it was clear that the fish were prepared to take an imitation fly if presented properly. They were clearly shy of any thicker line – interest was there, but would turn away as they nosed the fly.

So then it was off to North Wales for a week of salmon, grayling and brown trout fishing on the River Dee. I was renting a cottage a short drive from the river and meeting up the following day with Millie, who was also staying at the same location on a B&B basis.

The river was running high, which was good for the salmon fishing, but as salmon fishing goes it is very much a hit and miss situation. There were one or two showing themselves as they moved up river to spawn higher up the system later in the year, but they were very coloured and had been in the river for a while.

Millie was already waiting for me on Chain Pool at 7 am on the Monday morning as pre-arranged. Keen as mustard after an early start, he had brought with him a huge array of different rods, and I suspected he had included his Tenkara. I hate the very notion of those things and take the mickey out of him at every opportunity I can when he uses it.

As sure as eggs are eggs, out of the car boot it came and with a big grin on his face he set it up for grayling fishing. Not to be outdone, I set up my 11ft #4 for grayling and for a bit of a challenge I set up my #7 Trout rod for salmon. I wasn't over-confident about hooking up with a salmon, but a quick run through wouldn't hurt. Not surprisingly I blanked on the salmon front, but between us we picked off a few grayling on the lighter gear.

A brew and a sausage and egg butty from Yum Yums went down well as we sat outside debating which beat to visit next. We spent a pleasant half hour in the quiet town centre.

Deciding to stay local for the day we visited the town beats, where again we picked off a few grayling and wild browns, but they were only small. However, the size didn't matter, it was a pleasure just to be there.

We made an early start the following morning with Millie forgoing his breakfast, and set off for a beat that neither of us had visited before. Coed Yr Allt near Halton looked an interesting beat from the club brochure. Following the written directions to the upper end of the beat, we came across the farm tracks leading down towards the river. It had appeared quite accessible from the photos in the brochure, but we soon realised that they must have been taken some years ago. Accessible yes, with a 4x4 Jeep or tractor! But with my little Vauxhall Combo van – no chance! Having driven down the wrong track and nearly grounded the underside of the van, the only way back was to reverse all the way up the steep hill with some speed, hoping not to get stuck in the process. Somehow we managed to find the parking area, which again bore no resemblance to the photos in the brochure.

The van was absolutely plastered with mud up to the roof. Even the windscreen was splattered and goodness knows what damage I had incurred to the tyres and exhaust, but at least there were no visible dents or scratches to the paintwork.

The directions said to proceed on foot down a quad track to the river. Ha ha! It was a steep, narrow and barely used footpath that was overgrown, muddy and treacherously slippery, and both of us had to hang on to a roped handrail that had been installed by the club. We laughed all the way down, and it was a miracle neither of us ended up on our backsides. We were relieved to arrive at the bankside without broken legs. We discovered it was a beat that was only suitable for spinning on such high water levels – the river was pushing through at a right rate of knots.

By now neither of us were in the frame of mind to bother with the spinner, so we made a hasty retreat back to the mud-camouflaged van to tackle the vehicular assault course back to Halton and find our way to the lower end of the beat. We spent another 30 minutes driving around the Welsh countryside, taking several wrong turns. We finally arrived at the parking area, having driven about 15 miles to get 500 yards downriver. At least the access roads were a little more vehicle friendly.

With a hop, skip and a jump down the hill to the water's edge, we finally got to wet a line about three hours after leaving our digs. Millie was using his switch rod and I my #7 for salmon or sea trout. After a couple of hours' non-stop casting all I had to show was a lost sea trout of about 1lb and a small but beautifully-marked brown trout. Millie fared somewhat less well. Not only did he blank, he somehow snapped his rod clean in half on a bush!

It was time for another half-hour drive back to the Town beats in Corwen for a few casts at the grayling, just to finish the day off. We caught a few small fish during the afternoon and it was a relief to realise that no damage had occurred to the undercarriage of the van during the off-road trek, so it was not a completely disastrous day.

The next day we fancied a visit to another river in the area, a little tributary of the Alwen called the Afon Ceirw. Before setting off for the river we paid a visit to the car wash to get the van cleaned up. The attendant laughed and charged me only £6 for a thorough wash.

Tackling up at the bridge over the Ceirw, the clear water looked perfect, with glides, riffles and pools where we could try a cast for some brown trout. Millie went on downstream and when some time later we met up again, he was cock-a-hoop that he had caught one and I had blanked. I didn't even see a fish in half a mile of river. I suspect Millie had spooked them as he walked down the high bank before me. Well, that's my excuse anyway.

Walking upstream from the bridge, I saw a small brown rise to a fly in the first pool I came to. I changed my nymph for a small CDC Emerger and cast to the spot and the fish instantly rose to it and woofed it down and was hooked. Only about six or seven ounces, but it was a triumph to target what would turn out to be the only fish of the session, and indeed it was the only fish I saw. Millie had no luck on this stretch.

All was not lost though, as I learned an important lesson. On the walk back through the field I phoned Llyn Brenig Trout fishery to book both of us on for the following day. Unknown to me at the time the van keys dropped out of my pocket as I lifted out the phone, and on arrival at the van they were nowhere to be found. Oops!

Millie and I exchanged a few expletives as we set off, retracing my footsteps through the field, and I have to admit I was starting to panic a little, but luckily I found them after 10 minutes of searching. We both sighed with relief. I won't be making that mistake again of putting my keys in the same pocket as my phone.

Deciding to revisit the town waters again whilst discussing the error of my ways, we arrived at the road bridge in time for the mandatory brew and doughnut before setting off across the fields to our chosen pools in search of larger grayling and brown trout. But once again only the little ones were present. We anglers always say "size doesn't matter" when we don't catch a big one.

The next morning gave us a bit of a respite from river fishing as we set off over the hills to Llyn Brenig, a man-made 920-acre lake. Bank fishing was not an option for us – it was a boat trip we fancied. Millie wanted to be captain and I was elected first mate (navigator). Fully loaded and sporting rather less than fetching buoyancy aids, we cast off and motored towards the dam wall, where there were several fish rising.

Millie chose the Blob and I the "Drowned Daddy" as

starting flies, on #7 rods and 7lb leaders straight through to the fly. Apparently these fish were hard-fighting due to the cold, deep water. It wasn't long before Millie had a fish on and it certainly lived up to its reputation by fighting hard, even though it was only about 2lb when it finally came to the net. Within a couple of hours Millie had had five fish to my one – my "Daddy" method clearly wasn't working, although I had earlier been advised by the fishery manager that it would.

It was time for a rethink over a brew and a custard doughnut. Well that worked, as the fish stopped rising and Millie stopped catching, while I began to pick up a few on a variety of small lures and nymphs. Millie had a blank spell of about four hours before netting a couple more later on in the afternoon, as did I.

Millie finished the day with seven and I managed five, while both of us missed or released a few at distance. All were rainbows of similar size between 2lb and 2½ lb.

Our final day of the week on the Dee arrived only too soon, and we headed off in the van upstream from Chain Pool for the last time. Once again setting up for grayling on my 11ft #4 rod I picked off a few, but they were small ones again. Before calling it a session I suggested having another run through Chain Pool on the way back to the van. These last-minute decisions can make or break a day when confidence is at its lowest ebb and everything else has all but failed. Then a jolt on the rod tip indicated that a larger fish had taken the nymph and a bend in the rod confirmed that this was no tiddler. Although not a monster, it felt like a decent grayling, but the pull on the line indicated otherwise. After a few seconds a nice wild brown trout hit the surface, and I soon slid it over the waiting net. It was a fin perfect and beautifully marked "spotty" of 1½lb.

Shortly after that Millie landed his biggest grayling of the week on his, dare I say it, Tenkara rod. I found it highly amusing watching him attempt to land it with a fixed leader twice as long as his rod! The grayling had other ideas about being photographed by making a premature leap to freedom before I could get the camera ready.

However, the grayling was not the only thing of Millie's making a bid for freedom. A sudden gust of wind caught him by surprise, launching his cap into the water, far enough out of reach for him not to be able to retrieve it. It then promptly sunk. I had more laughs at Millie's expense in those final 10 minutes than the entire morning.

In the afternoon it was a return trip to the town waters, where once again the brew and doughnut ritual was performed and the landing of a few smaller grayling and brown trout brought the fishing to a close.

OCTOBER

A leisurely four-hour drive brought me to Glensherup Trout Fishery, a windswept 29-acre loch nestling in the Perthshire hills surrounded by stunningly beautiful scenery.

I had last been there a little over 12 months ago, sneaking in a couple of hours during a long weekend break with my wife.

When full the loch is about 55ft deep in the middle, but once again it was 10ft or so below its peak capacity. This made the whole loch accessible to the intrepid bank angler, although the terrain required stealth and a degree of balance that would challenge a circus acrobat.

I arrived a little before 10 o'clock and was greeted excitedly by a couple of very friendly resident canines. Already there were several anglers setting off in the boats. The fishery manager asked if I had an electric outboard engine with me if I wanted to take a boat out, so I had a look in the back of my van amongst all the other paraphernalia I was carrying with me and lo and behold... no I didn't. I hadn't planned on using a boat, as my prime objective was to walk the circumference of the Loch and get an idea of its contours and fish-holding areas, if I could find them of course.

The conditions were very similar to those of a year ago. I knew where a likely spot would be to catch a fish or two, and that was over on the far bank in the top corner by the dam wall. By the time I was geared up there were eight boats out on the water, but surprisingly they were not all together. There were four at the bottom end and four at the top end, disappointingly close to the banks where I was hoping to begin, taking into account the prevailing wind, which was blowing in from the south west towards the dam wall.

The usual discussion with the fishery manager confirmed my thoughts on fish location and also the flies that should work. No change then from my previous visit. I set up two rods, one with a floating line and a long leader with three equally-spaced buzzers and the other with an intermediate line and single Damsel Nymph.

As I gingerly made my way round to the far bank, carefully negotiating the rocks and shingle on the steep dam wall, I tried a cast or two, but it was quite pointless against the strong wind. I spotted a fish a couple of feet down about 20ft out and cast to it with the Damsel, to no avail as the fish slunk away into the depths of the comparatively clear water.

I saw one of the boat anglers net a fish on a fly I assumed to be a buzzer, judging by the way he was fishing. When I finally arrived at the east bank another boat angler was netting a fish, which encouraged me to think that the fish were following the wind and this was where my best chances would be.

Several casts with the buzzers produced nothing, so I changed size and colour, trying alternative variations until I had a take on a single small black epoxy buzzer fished quite shallow. I lifted the rod on the take into nothing, wondering what had happened. I spent a good hour spent in this area with no result, and even the boat anglers were beginning to rove about with frustration. I decided to change to a black CDC emerger and almost instantly had a rise, but didn't connect with anything. This happened three times before I actually latched on to a fish, only for it to throw the barbless hook when it jumped clear of the water. Then nothing for half an hour, so I decided to meander on round the loch, casting in likely spots where it was actually possible to get near to the water. Realising my balance was not what it used to be when I was 21, I didn't take any undue risks. The banks seemed to disappear vertically at the water's edge into the darkness of the depths and I didn't fancy an early bath.

I made my way all around to the most southerly point of the loch which took a couple of hours, just casting out here and there, with no indications from any fish whatsoever. Negotiating the little stream at the point of the Loch (incidentally I was quite proud of myself for not getting my feet wet), I made it to where the other boat anglers were anchored and it was here I made my first error of judgement with my foothold, and down I went onto the rocks. A strong Scottish-accented voice bellowed across the water from one of the boats, "are you alright mate"? "Yeah, I'm fine, nothing broken," I replied in my rather subdued and embarrassed dulcet southern tones. Picking myself up and dusting myself down, I enquired how the fishing was at this end of the loch, and it appeared not to be good with many of them blanking. So I didn't hang around but carried on with my trek. Finally I got back to where I had begun, still with no fish to my name, so I returned to the east bank to finish out the session. I was the only angler on the bank, and I could now see why.

The boat anglers at this end were very disgruntled, as they were struggling with only a handful of fish between them. I persevered with the CDC and was getting some more interest but still missing many rises. I lost another fish before netting and releasing this 3lb rainbow, being careful to keep it up from the stony shore.

So there it was, two lost fish, many, many missed rises and one in the net. Not the day I had expected, but nevertheless enjoyable. On the way back to the lodge my legs were getting a bit shaky from negotiating the rough terrain for four hours. I was certainly looking forward to getting back to the hotel to get fed and watered. I had eaten and drunk nothing since breakfast at Gretna Services early that morning.

Before I left I had a debriefing session with the fishery manager, who himself had been out on one of the boats and confirmed that the day had not been a good one. Our tactics had been very similar with identical results and there were a few anglers that had blanked, but that's what angling is all about and why it is so infectious, because the next time could be the best session ever, you just don't know.

After a ten-minute drive to Tormaukin Hotel in Glendevon, I checked in, and following an excellent hearty meal and a drink at the bar I settled down for the night. I awoke the next morning to clear skies and brilliant sunshine, and was looking forward to the drive to Morphie Dyke on the North Esk near Montrose for another experience of salmon fishing.

An hour and a half later I was at the fishery lodge, where I was introduced to the resident ghillie, Eric. As I was a novice at this game, Eric set up my gear for me, and eager to learn as much as possible, I asked many questions and he was more than happy to answer in great detail.

He took me straight off to the Dyke pool, the top pool of the beat and the one that all anglers want to get on, as it is where the fish rest before they run the Dyke itself. He pointed out all the areas where the fish rest up and then swim upstream from the lower pool. It was amazing to see the number of fish leaping from the water to gain position from the other fish in readiness to move on up the river. The man-made fish ladder at the Dyke had been dry for much of the summer because of the lack of rain on the east coast of Scotland.

After half an hour at this pool he was happy with my casting and suggested we should move further downriver to make way for other anglers wanting to fish this pool. It's salmon-fishing protocol to make way after about an hour or so at any given pool, if other anglers are waiting to move in. Eric assured me it that it's a good idea to move on even if there are no other anglers waiting, just to rest the pool.

As Eric introduced me to the other pools, I cast to the areas where he said would most likely hold fish. The fish were showing themselves, and I could actually see them under the water with my recently purchased Ray Ban polarised sunglasses. The water was very clear, and it was amazing to see all the rocks that would not otherwise be visible; I could see where the fish generally would hold up. In many areas I was able to wade right across the river, so I could spot the deeper holes where the current was not so strong. I was in my element. At that moment I wasn't bothered about catching a fish, as I was learning so much from such an experienced chap.

For the rest of the afternoon I was under Eric's wing, moving from pool to pool along the top half of the fishery. Not surprisingly I didn't catch anything, although I stayed on until dusk, long after Eric had packed away and gone home.

Accommodation was in the fishery house, where most of the group were staying, and Brian was cooking us all a chicken stew, with his very own hand-cut chips of course. Alcoholic beverages were free-flowing that night, but everyone was tired, so bedtime was reasonably early, ready for an early rise next morning.

Thursday morning couldn't come quick enough for me and I didn't get a great deal of sleep, mostly due to everyone else in the house snoring their heads off, especially the guy in the adjacent room. I wonder who that could have been... A mug of coffee revitalised me at first light and off to the river without any breakfast I went. I wasn't hungry, and even if I had been, I was far too excited to notice. It was a beautiful morning with blue sky and the rising sun in the east made me feel privileged to be where I was.

Eric arrived at 9 am and gave me some more advice, and I fished and fished all morning without so much as a knock on the line. The fish were still coming up the river, leaping and jumping in line as far down the river as I could see. It was just fantastic to witness this spectacle of nature, something I had never seen before, although Eric told me that because of the low water level they were not running up in the usual numbers from the sea. There were fish from just a few pounds to what looked to be over 20 pounds. I'm sure they were just laughing at me standing there with my rod in hand.

I was now fishing the Cage Pool and decided to change tactics from the fly to the toby lure. I had only had a few casts when just after one o'clock Brian drove past on his way to have some lunch and asked how I was getting on. I replied I'd scored a big fat zero and he drove off smiling.

He was only a couple of hundred yards down the track when I had my first yank on the line and a hook up. It took me so much by surprise that I nearly jumped out of my waders as the fish jumped just in front of me and tried to throw the hook. My heart missed a beat and I stood there in shock. After nearly 50 years of fishing, all that knowledge instantly left me me and I hadn't a clue what to do. I just hung for dear life, not wanting to lose my rod as the fish tore off downstream at such a rate my reel was almost smoking.

Stupidly I hadn't flicked the anti-reverse mechanism on, and the handle was spinning round at a ridiculous rate of knots. I couldn't stop it at first and had to let it run until the fish slowed and I was able to stop and turn it. I was all fingers and thumbs – panicking was probably nearer the mark.

The fish eventually came back up the river and I played it for what seemed to be an eternity, though it was probably only five minutes in reality. By this time my heart was pumping out of my chest and I was shaking with excitement like a drunkard, stumbling on the rocks under my feet as I began to believe I might have caught my first salmon.

It was then I realised that I hadn't got a net, and there was no shallow gravel bank around for me to beach the fish. I attempted to draw it into the rocks close to the edge, where I was hoping to grab hold of its tail. It was a good silver salmon of about 12-15lb. I thought I had it beaten as it slowly glided towards me, but at the last second it flipped over on its side, gave a huge flip of its tail and the hook came free. The fish disappeared back out into the river with an explosive whirlpool.

I cannot put in writing how I felt and what I said to myself, but to say the least, I was absolutely gutted. I stood there cursing to myself and felt so alone, with no one there to console me. Only anglers know that feeling.

Still shaking from the exhilaration and disappointment of the nearly-but-not-quite experience, I went for a cuppa and spilled the news to the others who had gathered for lunch in the hut. It was then that Brian gave me a net. I returned to the same spot after my lunch break, brimming with expectation of another fish and casting my lure to the exact spot as before. Swinging it around at the same angle where I achieved my first hook up, it was only a few casts before I had my second hook up and a coloured fish of around 10lb came soaring out of the water. Again my heart pounded, but unfortunately my exaltation was short lived – I allowed the line to go far too slack and the fish was off. I cursed myself once again. Stupid, stupid, stupid!

Perseverance is the name of this game and I carried on regardless. After about half an hour I had my third hook up, from the very same spot as the other two. I thought there must be an area of water where they felt comfortable resting up in the fast-flowing current, probably behind a large boulder. This time the fish stayed down deep and fought with a slow, heavy plod. It felt huge. This time I maintained a tight line, but again the hook pulled free as the fish swam past me upstream. It was my fault yet again. I had previously got snagged on the bottom and had had to pull it free by tightening up the rear drag to its maximum. Not returning the drag to the correct tension was a schoolboy error on my part, and I paid the penalty when the hook pulled out. It was utterly amazing that after all the experience I had had in angling I could still make such basic errors, but it is quite common when experiencing something new that you forget everything you know in the excitement of the moment.

After a while the news spread of my failed angling skills and others were hankering after a go on this pool, so reluctantly I gave way as it was the right thing to liberate my so-called lead boots from the small plateau I had made with my feet in the stones.

I fished the day out moving up and down the beats and switching from fly to lure without any other signs of fish except the ones showing off by leaping right in front of me as if they were mimicking dolphins. I was still buzzing with excitement, but also feeling somewhat disappointed with myself, until hunger got the better of me and I returned to the house for some supper.

Friday saw a different weather system arrive with wind and drizzle sweeping across the landscape, but that didn't deter any of us from an early start. Still bitterly disappointed with myself, I picked the Cage Pool again and stayed there without so much as a touch until lunchtime, when it was time for me leave for my next port of call.

In summary, Eric said I had done well as a first-timer in difficult conditions, which made me feel a bit better. Incidentally, as far as I am aware, eight anglers fished and only one salmon of 6lb and a sea trout of about 1lb were landed in the three days of my visit.

NOVEMBER

For once I had a very pleasant drive down the M6 and M5 on my way down to Amesbury in Wiltshire. The roads were fairly quiet and the sun was shining, and for a change I was in no particular rush to get anywhere fast, except that I wanted to have a quick peek at Avon Springs trout fishery in Durrington before my session on the Wiltshire Avon chalkstream the following day.

I arrived at 2 pm, still enjoying the glorious sunshine, with 16 degrees and no wind. It felt more like one of those enjoyable spring days in April than depressing November with only the long, wet winter to look forward to. My mind was in turmoil: would I, could I, or even should I, have a few casts? I didn't want to take any fish, because I wasn't going home for a few days and it's a shame to kill for killing's sake.

Last cast was at 4 pm, or so it read on the board, but that doesn't mean much as anglers always have a minimum of 18 last casts and it wasn't going to get dark until about 5 pm. A word or two with the manager in the office/workshop about which flies had been working was inconclusive, but a fellow angler was just coming off the water and told me he had caught his quota on a large mayfly. A mayfly, in November? I looked at his fly and it resembled more of a drowned daddy Longlegs than a mayfly, which seemed much more plausible for this time of year.

Well, the temptation was too much to bear, so I gave in and paid my fees for a couple of hours' fishing. The odd fish was rising in the middle of Club Lake to what seemed to be midges, so I tied on a Daddy. Well, you would wouldn't you? There wasn't enough time to ponce about with small flies on five acres of water, I wanted the fish to see my fly immediately upon splashdown. Well that idea failed miserably and I persuaded myself to try something smaller. A Klinkhamer never fails to attract fish and amazingly enough a fish rose to my first cast, but I was so startled I struck about a week too late as the fish snatched my fly down into the crystal clear depths of the lake before my tiny brain could register that I had had a take. I put it down to the fact I was fatigued after the long drive and in any case I wasn't too bothered about catching. This happened once again during a quiet period when all signs of fish rising had ceased.

As the sun began to drop behind the trees a chill came over me, letting me know time was moving on. I changed my Klink to a nymph for the remaining twilight half hour, performing a fast roly-poly retrieve with intermittent pauses and receiving a couple of indications on the line from fish – or was it weed?

It was soon time to continue my journey to the hotel in Amesbury with a blank. I was more disappointed that the light had gone so much more quickly than I had wanted it to, but who cares? At least I had seen the venue and had a few casts to pacify that uncontrollable, urgent lust to wet a line that somehow anglers of all disciplines never seem to lose as they get older.

The next morning was much colder than recent mornings with a thick fog blanketing the countryside on the short drive back to Durrington. The weather forecast was once again good with plenty of sunshine and a slight breeze. Perfect for river fishing. The gates were still locked when I arrived, so I waited outside.

Dead on 8:30 the gates opened and that same old feeling of excitement came over me, just as it always has done since I was a young boy waiting to get down to my local stream near home.

I had a chat with the owner whilst changing into my waders, then, after having a coffee and a doughnut to start the day off, I tackled up my #5 Streamflex with a 4.5lb tapered leader and a 4.1lb tippet and attached my flashback Pheasant Tail Nymph for the grayling. Wading in general is not permitted here, but it is always advisable to wear waders when river fishing and in any case the short grass was soaked from the morning dew, and you never know when you may have to get down to the water's edge to release fish or just to avoid snagging your line whilst playing a fish.

With a spring in my step I soon found myself at the bottom end of the beat. The water was lower than its normal winter level, consisting mostly of shallow riffles at this end. Highly oxygenated water is the prime habitat for grayling. I couldn't see any fish in this clear fast-flowing water, but I knew there must be some hiding somewhere in the stony bottom.

It wasn't long before I felt my first take from a fish and struck into a solid resistance from an out-of-season wild brown trout. Oops! Here we go again. I changed my flashback PTN to a tiny tungsten bead PTN and began getting small grayling at the rate of one every two or three casts for a while, but they too were tiny and I did really want something a bit bigger.

I changed to a caddis nymph, which brought fewer but larger fish to the bank. As I continued upstream I approached an inlet from the trout farm and instantly spooked a huge fish from the shallow glide, but this was definitely not a grayling.

Several casts here returned a few more small grayling and another little brown trout. I needed to locate the larger grayling that I had been told were present, so I began stalking instead of just speculating while casting. I only saw one of about 3lb which was impossible to cast to as it was underneath an overhanging shrub that was touching the surface in between two trees. I waited for several minutes, watching its movements, but it wasn't going to come out of its own free will so I moved on. There was no point in spooking it out, as fish rarely take a fly when spooked.

By now I was more than half way up the one-mile stretch and still had only seen the one large grayling, so I resorted back to speculative casting, picking up more small ones and yet another little brownie. Reaching the end of the beat where the water was slower and deeper, I had only seen one very large brown trout and several small grayling by the time a lunch break was due.

Back to the car park for a brew, another doughnut and a welcome rest. Sitting on the banks of the river watching nature is the most idyllic way to spend a lunchtime for me. My mind just wanders, and everything is good with the world. Well, in my world anyway, and when you're out fishing nothing else matters.

Suddenly I found I was not alone. A flock of seagulls appeared from nowhere and began swooping down on the river. A swan was slurping at the surface and fish began to rise everywhere. There were several big fish breaking the surface regularly all over the pool and for several minutes it was absolute pandemonium.

The reason soon became clear when the owner returned from the fish farm, having fed pellets to his stock in the rearing pond. The rearing pond is fed by an offshoot from the main river further upstream and flows out at the top of this pool. Some of the pellets float out with the flow back into the river, providing this bonus feed for all that swims and flies. I would never have believed how many fish were in this pool had I not witnessed this chaotic feeding frenzy for myself.

After all the pellets had been consumed the seagulls flew off, the swan continued its journey upstream and the fish returned to wherever they had come from. So just where had they all come from, and where did they all go?

After my lunch there was only one place for me to fish. I couldn't see any fish at all but clearly they were there and they were in a feeding mood. A change of fly from the small nymph to a larger morsel, a beaded Squirmy Wormy, was hastily made. Blind upstream casting close in was the starting point and I would fan out my casts across the pool as I made my way up to the inlet.

Only a few casts in, I felt what I initially thought was the bottom, but on the strike it bolted off upstream. Quite a tussle ensued as the fish tore up and down and then up to the inlet again, with me just hanging on. In turn I was up and down the banks trying to keep in touch at all times, wading through the weed to keep the fish away, until in open water it eventually tired and began to come to the surface. This was no minnow. I failed at the first attempt at landing it, but then, with both of us tiring, I beached it on the weed and scooped it up in the net. It weighed 6lb exactly.

Totally dishevelled following my antics running around the bank, I triumphantly posed with my catch for a photo by the owner, who proclaimed "I told you there were some big 'uns in there". The fight took a lot out of the fish and I had to hold it for several minutes in the current before its strength returned and it could swim away safely.

Pleased as punch with my biggest ever river-caught brown trout (albeit out of season) I carried on casting in the same pool. After picking up a couple of larger grayling, I changed the Squirmy to a beaded Hare's Ear nymph and rested the pool for a few minutes. There were plenty more fish in there to be caught and I was sure I could get one or two more before it was time to go.

I thought about dropping the nymph into the head of the glide where I had spooked the big fish in the morning. Of course it could well have been the fish I had just caught, but my thinking was that where there is one there may be another.

I was right. A fish took the nymph as it landed in the shallows, then turned 180 degrees and took off into the deeper water. Another fight was on and it was pretty much the same up and down tug of war fight that the other one had given me. It was a fish of similar size – surely it couldn't be the same one? As it came to the surface it was clear that it was a different fish, and once again it took me a couple of stabs before it went in the net. It weighed slightly under 6lb.

My arms were tired after casting and catching all day, but I finished the day on a high, and what a day it was, in a beautiful setting with excellent fishing. I decided I would definitely be back, and next time it would be during the trout season.

Heading off the following morning to Hampshire, I fancied a day's catch and release at Meon Springs. This is one of very few fisheries in the south of England that operate catch and release. That morning I arrived shortly after 8:30 am and there was nobody about, so I signed in and drove off to the lower two pools, which are catch and release only. Having been there before I didn't bother to look at the pools and just tackled up as per my previous visit, a #5 rod and reel and small nymph on a 10ft tapered leader.

Fully attired and looking forward to a good day's sport, I quietly approached the end pool. Imagine my disappointment when I got to the water's edge to find both pools covered with thick blanket weed. Only one small area had been cleared for fishing in each pool. There was no way I was going to waste a few hours thrashing about in two areas which were not much larger than your average garden goldfish pond. I wasn't going to embarrass myself by even wetting a line, so I put my rod back in the van and went back to sign out. By this time the fishery manager was in the office with other anglers, and I expressed my dissatisfaction to everyone and left. What a shame the management couldn't maintain those two pools to the same standards as the others.

Back in the van, I pondered on where to go next and after much deliberation over several possibilities I decided to go to Chalk Springs in West Sussex, a venue I have fished many times before.

There is no catch and release here, but I was sure I could do long distance release on a few fish as well as land a few. Arriving at 10 am, I chose a three-fish ticket which would also allow me up to seven hours' fishing if I so wished, prolonging the day by stalking particular specimens. It is quite possible to reach a quota within minutes at this venue, but there is not a lot of point in doing that, so fish selection is the way to go.

The fishery always looks good and is well managed, with rearing and stock pools providing a mouth-watering spectacle of provocative and tantalising sights as you walk past on your way to the four beautifully-manicured lakes.

Bypassing North Lake (it looked far too easy), I spotted a couple of fish at the top end of West Lake. Once again armed with my #5 rod and reel, I cast my PTN in the general direction of the cruising fish. They both showed interest in the nymph as I pulled it away from a smaller, more aggressive rainbow which would have devoured the fly if allowed. I cast again to the larger of the two and instantly it surged towards the nymph and it was on, and a fight ensued. My first fish of the day was in the bag. One down, two to go, and I had only been fishing five minutes.

Leaving West Lake, I moved on to East Lake and walked all the way around, looking for some larger specimens to stalk.

There was one sandy-coloured rainbow of about 5-6lb near the surface and I set myself up to target this fish for a while. Cast after cast in front of it brought no interest from the fish, which totally ignored my offering. I spent about 30 minutes targeting this fish but it wasn't having any of it, so I left it alone for a while and ventured over to South Lake.

Both pools were flat calm, which made it harder to land a nymph without making a disturbance on the surface which would make the fish aware that something was not quite right. Several other anglers were casting their lines on the water, and this was obviously making the fish cautious as to what was natural and what wasn't. I gave up on the stalking tactic, as this was clearly not working, and resorted to a copper PTN much deeper down.

The sun was dropping behind the trees and dark shadows were being cast across the pools. The fish moved deeper, which was exactly where I wanted them, and it wasn't long before my second fish came to the net. I had about four hours left on the clock, so there was plenty of time to get my last fish. Time for a brew, a doughnut and a general walk around searching for larger fish. I couldn't find anything larger than I had already caught, as by now the fish in South and East Lakes had all but disappeared. I moved up to West Lake, where a few fish were still moving around in the mid-afternoon sunshine. The fishery keeper joined me and during our conversations I hooked and lost two at distance, blaming it on my lack of concentration whilst chatting. He went on his way laughing. Half an hour later I began to get a little bored, so after paying more attention to what I should be doing, I soon picked up my third and final fish of the day.

I called into the cleaning room on the way back to weigh and record my catch and the three fish weighed 7.3lb.

DECEMBER

The first proper frosts of the year brought freezing conditions to Clay Lane, with ice forming at the top end of the pool and a light dusting of snow making for a seasonal picture. These conditions had put the fish right down for the best part of the day, with only one or two making a brief appearance when the sun shone in the middle of the day.

Kieran used his trusty Cat's Whisker for a while without success, changing to an Orange Fritz, which teased a couple of rainbows into reacting the way they should, or at least the way we would like them to. I managed four on an unweighted bloodworm fished on a sinking line and one on a Corixa fished midwater, which really surprised me, but I have to try all sorts.

The fishing wasn't that brilliant on the one and only occasion we visited the fishery, so Kieran thought it would be a good idea to help out at a bit of shepherding.

A trip down to Sussex for a few days was an excuse to pinch a couple of hours at Chalk Springs at Arundel. The air temperature dropped to -3 during the night and the likelihood of ice could have jeopardised my plans. However, the fishery being fed from natural chalk springs (hence its name), the water emerges at a constant 10 degrees, so it has to be a severe cold spell for the waters to freeze completely, unlike other stillwater fisheries. I signed in and chose the three-fish ticket option. As it was cold the fish would be ok in the back of the van for a couple of days until I got home to Stockport.

A doughnut and a warm mug of hot coffee soon got my circulation going on this frosty morning as I set up my #5 rod ready for some stalking. My favourite flashback Pheasant Tail Nymph was my first choice of fly.

Passing by North Pool, as I usually do – it's far too easy in this little pool – I decided to begin on West Pool. There were three anglers already fishing the nearside bank, so I walked around to the far side and spotted a brownie lurking around about three feet down. It was quite long but didn't look very fat. Nonetheless I crouched down and flicked my nymph several feet past its nose, allowing it to sink a little before drawing it back toward the fish. The fish saw the fly and lunged towards it, and with no hesitation I struck and the fish was on. It wasn't much of a fight, with no more than a short downward lunge, then a twist and a turn as it came to the surface and into my waiting net. It was quite a pretty fish for the time of year, even though it was very lean. It had been stocked in the summer and almost certainly would have been much heavier and put up a more lively fight had it been caught at that time. To the other anglers, I must have looked as though I knew what I was doing with my one cast, one fish strategy. Just lucky I guess!

Bypassing South Pool, because I couldn't see any fish and it was partly iced over at the far end in the shade of the trees, I moved onto East Pool, where I spotted a good sandy-coloured fish wallowing around under a tree.

It was moving round and round in a circle under the over-hanging branches that fell close to the surface of the water and impossible to cast under. However, there was a slight gap which I thought I might be able to flick my nymph into, teasing the fish towards it on the retrieve. Again, kneeling down, I waited for a few minutes for the fish to return on its repetitive journey. When it was facing in my direction, I flicked the nymph out. The fish moved towards it but didn't take it. I repeated this several times, watching the fish closely – in the event of it showing any further movement to the nymph I would strike in anticipation of a take. After half an hour of unsuccessful attempts and a few changes of nymph pattern It didn't happen, so I rested it for a while, moving on up the pool.

Seeing two fish cruising in the sunshine near the surface of the middle of the pool, I cast over to them with my flashback

Pheasant Tail Nymph and one of them, without looking twice at the fly, snaffled it down with a huge commotion. It put up a good fight for several minutes before being finally brought to the net. The tussle spooked several other fish, so I moved back round to the tree to see if the sandy rainbow was still there. It was. Resuming my awkward stance, I cast again and again without receiving a definitive take from the fish. I was beginning to think of giving up, as my knees were getting colder and wetter, but then I decided to try something a little larger in an attempt to attract the fish's attention. I changed my nymph to a beadhead bloodworm, working it from the bottom upwards as the fish moved towards me.

It worked. The fish lunged toward the fly, and I struck as I saw it open its mouth, impaling the hook into its jaw. It was quite a lump compared to the other two fish I caught earlier as it put a good bend into my #5 Streamflex rod. Eventually it came to the net and a fellow angler offered to be photographer for me and the fish. I weighed it at just under 6lb in the net.

That was to be my final bit of action for the day. It was now back to the weighing room to wash and gut my catch. According to the scales the three fish weighed a combined 12lb 6ozs while the sandy rainbow only weighed 4lb 14ozs. How strange!

To finish off the year, Millie and I took a trip to Corwen to fish for grayling on the River Dee. It took a little longer to get there because we were met by a blizzard on the A5 all the way from Chirk roundabout. After nearly losing control of the van and skidding into a brick wall, we finally arrived on Chain Pool.

The doughnuts and coffee made a welcome respite following nearly two hours of driving. The temperature was − 0.5 degrees, but the wind chill factor made it feel like at least -5.

An 11ft #4 rod with a couple of nymphs was my set-up for the day. Arriving at the pool, I found the water was pushing through, slightly coloured and rising. It was going to be tough going in these conditions and I only managed two grayling and dropped one, while Millie fluked one and dropped it.

But when the fish aren't biting, there is always the wildlife to watch when you are waist deep in bitterly-cold water. You know it's time to get out when after an hour in the water your legs begin to tingle and go numb as the blood vessels shut down and the circulation begins to stop, just before hypothermia sets in. But it's all in a day's fishing, and I love it.

The best bit is warming up again in the local café with a breakfast bap and a coffee. Millie found a new friend to share his tales of woe with, although I thought the Pixie was giving me the look of love.

Following the short break we moved on to the town waters, where Millie winkled out a small grayling on his wretched Tenkara before we called it a day, bringing another eventful year of fishing to an end.

CHAPTER 13

From the Heart of Frank Sawyer

I never got to meet Frank Sawyer, but I did have the pleasure of the company of his son Tim for a day on the River Avon at Upavon in Wiltshire, more commonly known to us fly fishers as Frank's back garden. For this area was where the great nymph angler and wildlife trapper invented his famous Pheasant Tail Nymph, known to anglers around the world as one of the most successful flies ever. Frank was also well known locally for inventing rabbit traps.

Tim proudly spoke of his father's love of the river where he was the keeper at Netheravon, a little further downstream from where we were fishing. Back in those days grayling were classified as vermin, a pest to the trout angler, so a catch and kill policy was introduced to control the ever-increasing numbers. Dry fly-fishing caught a few grayling, but Frank needed to catch them much faster. He studied the main diet of the grayling by opening the stomachs of his catch to identify the digested insects. He would then catch live insect nymphs and keep them in pools so he could observe their behaviour and imitate them with an artificial fly. He invented the generic Pheasant Tail Nymph, tied with fine copper wire and pheasant-tail fibres, and then the Killer Bug, tied specifically to catch grayling.

Tim began to tell me how Frank introduced him to angling at the tender age of three. Tim would sit upon his father's shoulders learning how to cast and catch the numerous grayling at their feet, often returning home with a bag of 50 fish to turn into animal feed or fertiliser. Frank's love for the river had also begun at an early age and his childhood dream was to work and manage his local chalkstream, the Avon. Like many young boys of that time he couldn't wait to leave school, and by the age of 14 he announced that he wanted to give up mainstream education to work on the land. Later in life he took up writing, helped by Sir Grimwood Mears, who asked him to write a poem as an exercise to demonstrate his grasp of language. The result was The Chalk Stream, which I reproduce here with permission.

THE CHALK STREAM

High in the hills amid the chalk, I saw the light of day
Slowly along with murmured song, I gently wind my way.
Into the valley, green and gay, I creep with pride and stealth

Just Me and the Fish

I bring with me, for all to see, great happiness and wealth.
My friends come running from afar, given birth by tiny springs
O'er gravel bright I run in fright, with dread lest hindered be,
My journey, nay, no thing shall stay, is downward to the sea.

Through towns and farms and villages, past cottages and mills,
I give good health with all my wealth, to all who have the wills.
I give my life that all may hire, a share to everyone
With burdens great and burdens small, I help my friend the sun.
I gather strength with every yard, my wealth I shower with glee
I increase in rate with every spate, no one shall hinder me.
O'er gravel bright I run in fright, with dread lest hindered be,
My journey, nay, no thing shall stay, is downward to the sea.

Through sluice and hatch, o'er dam and weir, through meads and watering places
My waters great rush as in spate, as on the mill wheel races.
Gently throughout the meads I creep, enriching as I go
The produce fine will feed the kine in days of frost and snow.
Down from the hills with eyes agleam the thirsty cattle run
From dust and flies and cloudless skies, to shadow from the sun.
O'er gravel bright I run in fright, with dread lest hindered be,
My journey, nay, no thing shall stay, is downward to the sea.

Algae green, so seldom seen, whose life the sun has started
On weed and stone they make their home, until by me are parted.
The tiny young of many flies, of midges and sedges too,
Swim on and out or crawl about, with nothing else to do.
The nymphs swim quickly from my bed, and to the surface rise
A caddis face pokes out from its case as on my bed it lies.
O'er gravel bright I run in fright, with dread lest hindered be,
My journey, nay, no thing shall stay, is downward to the sea.

Mike Fox

The snails come creeping through the mud in swarms to lay their eggs

A shrimp with lady in his arms, a mass of moving legs.

Low in my bank and under stones, the horny crayfish skulks,

The big female, under whose tail her eggs, in number bulks.

A lamprey struggles to and fro, its mouth full up with stones,

The blue head worms with crooks and squirms retreat into their homes.

O'er gravel bright I run in fright, with dread lest hindered be,

My journey, nay, no thing shall stay, is downward to the sea.

A boatman flits from stem to stem, its belly to the sky

Black spiders lean, walk on my stream, can neither swim nor fly.

The daddy-long-legs creep about, as ugly in the air

And brown and bluey dragon-flies leave me to fly and pair.

The running newt and crawling toad, to all I give a place

Into the bog comes croaking frog to propagate his race.

O'er gravel bright I run in fright, with dread lest hindered be,

My journey, nay, no thing shall stay, is downward to the sea.

For fishes great and fishes small, their food I must produce

A store for all, in spring, in fall, for stickleback and luce.

For minnows decked in fine array, for loach and bullheads too,

For eel and pout, who range about from dark until morning dew.

For roach and dace who love the sun and gather in a school.

For tench and rudd, deep in the mud at the bottom of the pool

O'er gravel bright I run in fright, with dread lest hindered be,

My journey, nay, no thing shall stay, is downward to the sea.

I have the food for lordly trout and weeds to make a hide

No grayling waits for long in vain in gravel run or glide.

Neath trees that weep towards my deep I feed the perch and chub

Just Me and the Fish

With luckless fish, or if they wish, with caddis fly or grub.
Into the deep I gently creep with slowly running stream.
I bring enough to feed the ruffe, the barbel and the bream.
O'er gravel bright I run in fright, with dread lest hindered be,
My journey, nay, no thing shall stay, is downward to the sea.

The aimless gudgeons creep about, and dig with bearded snout
Expose the creeper and the worms where e'er they seek or rout.
I foster plants upon my bed, in deep, in glide, in run
From bed to face, while on I race, their arms reach to the sun.
I give them beauty, food and life, that they may too, in turn
Give shelter, food and breath of life to fishes, fly and worm.
O'er gravel bright I run in fright, with dread lest hindered be,
My journey, nay, no thing shall stay, is downward to the sea.

I find the food for waterfowl and cover for their eggs
For heron grey, at close of day, bent neck and outstretched legs.
The wild duck hidden in the rush, her brood she quickly brings
And little grebe in time of need hide chicks within her wings.
The moorhen scuttling from my side and coot with whitened face
And tiny rail, and snipe, and teal, for all I find a place.
O'er gravel bright I run in fright, with dread lest hindered be,
My journey, nay, no thing shall stay, is downward to the sea.

The kingfisher, with flash of blue and quickly beating wings
Will whistle clear for all to hear, the only note it sings.
A dipper flits from stone to stone and dives beneath my race
Some food I find, of many a kind, no matter what my pace.
To noble swan and bittern rare I offer weeds and fish,
To cormorant and little tern, to eat as they would wish.

Mike Fox

O'er gravel bright I run in fright, with dread lest hindered be,
My journey, nay, no thing shall stay, is downward to the sea.

I cater too for animals, give banks to make their holt
Make safe the vole and tiny shrew, as from stoat they bolt.
The otter dives into my pools and swims with lightning speed.
And grabs the tails of frightened trout, or eels from stone or weed.
In spring the old bitch brings her cubs to find the food themselves.
And teaches them to hunt my bed for crevices and shelves.
O'er gravel bright I run in fright, with dread lest hindered be,
My journey, nay, no thing shall stay, is downward to the sea.

Wagtail, finch and flycatcher, come near to make their nests
And feed on flies that from me rise, with many stops and rests.
The tireless swift flies up and down, with sand martin and swallow
And take my flies as they rise, too quick for me to follow.
The warblers run to join the fun, when flies have reached the rushes
My big mayflies, indeed a prize, for robins, wrens and thrushes.
O'er gravel bright I run in fright, with dread lest hindered be,
My journey, nay, no thing shall stay, is downward to the sea.

I give good sport to man and maid, no matter what their station.
Beauty I find to ease their mind in times of meditation.
The angler creeps with beating heart, high hopes to fill his creel
And with his wiles my fish beguiles with help of rod and reel.
With line of silk and cast so fine, with furred and feathered fly.
With lure or bait, they meet their fate, wherever they may lie.
O'er gravel bright I run in fright, with dread lest hindered be,
My journey, nay, no thing shall stay, is downward to the sea.

Just Me and the Fish

Onwards I go, past hill and dale, through trees and scrub and heather

Sometimes I rush in torrent great in cold and stormy weather.

I leave my bounds and wander far to fill the lowest places

The frightened mole comes from its hole, to higher land it races.

The shrew and vole from sodden nest, with cold their backs do hump

And swim with zest to place of rest inside a withy stump.

O'er gravel bright I run in fright, with dread lest hindered be,

My journey, nay, no thing shall stay, is downward to the sea.

My arms reach out on either side and trail back to their source

And bring their yields from other fields to aid me with their force.

My gravel bed I scour with glee, make bright the stream and drawn.

For salmon great and sea trout late come and lay their spawn.

I make a passage in the spring, for elver fresh from sea

Give food and hides, till, with silvered sides, they return in fall with me.

O'er gravel bright I run in fright, with dread lest hindered be,

My journey, nay, no thing shall stay, is downward to the sea.

I hasten steps with every mile, my waters great and wide.

I leave the valley, meads and hills, my bed my waters hide.

The life created on my run, I leave that they may too,

Give health and wealth and happiness to all who have the due.

Into the sea I quickly glide, through wave that gently smothers

I've had my run, my turn is done, in giving life to others.

O'er gravel bright I run in fright, with dread lest hindered be,

My journey fast has stopped at last, and I've won my victory.

Frank Sawyer